ACEs in the shadows
Understanding Adverse Childhood Experiences

By A. Survivor

I dedicate this book to my wonderful loving wife and family, and my collection trusted friends.

Thank you to The Cumbrian Wordsmith for proof reading this book and providing words of wisdom and reflection for the images.
https://uk.linkedin.com/in/lyn-osbaldeston-39937565

Cover by ThreeJays iStock: Getty Images

All other images by: Trudie Smith Photography
https://www.facebook.com/TrudieSmithPhotography/

Firstly, a thank you to the author for allowing me to add to the team supporting this area of need. I'm supporting the publication of the first 1000 copies of this book in memory of my brother Neil Jones whose personal struggle with his own adverse childhood experiences became too much.

In my career I have helped and assisted many children to identify and work out the impact of their life experiences on their past, present and future paths; each individual child brings their own story and through a greater understanding of 'ACEs' from us all we can help so many more to live life to the full.
Clare Houghton – Director. A Wilderness Way
http://www.awwltd.com

Contents:

1.   Preface

2.   What are ACEs?

3.   The ACEs Study

4.   The ACEs Movement

5.   How I Score 10 ACEs

6.   How ACEs affected my life

7.   How I am recovering from ACEs

8.   What can YOU do about ACEs?
      8a - Al Coates MBE
      8b - Judy James
      8c - Laura McConnell
      8d - A. Survivor

Links for research

ACEs Training

ACEs Questionnaire

1. Preface

Ok, I will start with a confession. I originally entitled this book 50 Shades of ACEs because I thought it would get some attention, and indeed it did. Social media gave an immediate judgement on the proposed title. Many people thought the title would either offend or even trigger people who have been affected by sexual abuse or exploitation; others thought it was fine.

However, the silent majority had the loudest voice in so far as they made no comment either way. As it happens I had more 'for' than 'against' comments but I decided to tone the title down, and from that decision I think I arrived at a more appropriate title and I guess it worked if you are reading this.

Sorry, but I am a creative entrepreneur as well as a 10 ACEs survivor and marketing is my thing.

My motto is "sell the sizzle not the bloody sausage".

That said, the 50 Shades of ACEs description is probably closer to the possible number of adverse childhood experiences we could each list than the more well-known 10 ACEs examples used in the original ACEs questionnaire study more than 20 years ago. On the other hand, I think ACEs in the shadows conveys an equally important point.

Adverse Childhood Experiences are often hidden and festering in the shadows of someone's life for many years; before having the light of scrutiny and understanding shone upon them.

Moving on, and just in case you have been living on the moon for the past year or so, here is a brief description of ACEs (Adverse Childhood Experiences) to keep you going until we get to the relevant chapters that follow.

The original ACEs Study was conducted at an American health maintenance organization Kaiser Permanente and the Centres for Disease Control from 1995 to 1997; there were two waves of data collection. More than 17,000 Health Maintenance Organization members from Southern California (yes, it's American but so is McDonalds) who were being assessed under physical examination, each completed confidential surveys regarding their childhood experiences and current health status and behaviours.

The study demonstrated beyond any reasonable doubt that there was an association of adverse childhood experiences (ACEs) (aka childhood trauma) with health and social problems across the lifespan. The study is frequently cited as a notable landmark in epidemiological research and has produced many scientific articles, conference and workshop presentations that examine ACEs and toxic stress.
So, why did I feel the need to write this small book you may ask?

The truth is that I thought to myself: Hey! I could write a book about ACEs.

I have at least 10 of them and that must make me an ACEs expert and maybe people will be interested in how I got 10 ACEs, how they affected (technical term for screwed-up) my life, and perhaps more importantly, how I am sustainably recovering from ACEs.

'By A. Survivor'. Yes, I am a survivor and that is all you need to know.

My name is irrelevant but my 60+ years of lived experience and my 'outside of the box' take on the whole ACEs phenomena, as I see it, may be of some interest to you. I hope so; otherwise you have wasted your money buying the book, but thanks anyway.

So, what the hell is this book all about?

It's intended to be a brief no-nonsense, straight talking, dumbed-down book about adverse childhood experiences and how "the shit that misses the fan, and hits you as a kid, can have a devastating effect on your life." My own quote.

It's dumbed down because I do not want to make it technical or so highly complicated that you need a degree to understand it. That type of analysis and explanation is already available to read if you prefer it.
At this point in writing I have no idea if I will meet that intention. I can only hope.

My second confession, before we get on with the book, is that I designed the cover and published it on social media before I wrote this preface.

I tend to do things my own way and often arse about tit, with the cart before the horse. It's just how my brain is wired.

I know this approach comes from having to endure adult sexual lust, gross violence, and abandonment (3 ACEs right there) while I was still learning to be a child.

You see, I had to find a way to survive the idiots in charge of my childhood and then overcome the adverse experiences they created around me.

This took a creative and somewhat unconventional approach to growing up as my brain rewired for survival while still developing.

I had to learn to navigate a route to adult life burdened with numerous obscured understandings of human beings and human nature and this also included the literal inability to trust anyone.

My trust button was not just broken, it was completely missing from my brain.

I guess my adult life, and all the complications it has entailed so far, has been lived at one hundred miles an hour with a firmly engrained mindset;

'I can trust no one, so I'll do it my way, and if they don't like it they can just f**k off.'

2. What are ACEs?

There is a list of World War II flying Aces that can be found on any internet search under the search term ACES. Fighter Aces in World War II had tremendously varying kill scores, affected as they were by many factors such as the pilot's skill level and the performance of the airplane he flew and those he flew against. Well that is not the ACEs list I will be referring to in this book.

There was a time in recent history when the Mario Tennis Aces would have listed on the first page results of a Google search, competing with the Las Vegas ACES women's basketball for the top spot.

If you search ACES right now, on any search engine, you will discover Adverse Childhood Experiences (ACEs).

That search phrase is now often winning the fight with Mario and Las Vegas for the top position.

If you happen on the Ace Cider company brand name, used by California Cider Company, enjoy the drinks but please don't get too drunk before you read the rest of this book.

I guess the search engine search for ACEs is the best demonstration to show how far the acronym ACEs has come since it was first used some 20 years ago by Doctors Felitti and Anda when completing the CDC-Kaiser Permanente Adverse Childhood Experiences (ACE) Study.

It now dominates page one of most search engines.

Yes, but what are ACEs? I hear you say. A C E s = Adverse Childhood Experiences.

The ACEs acronym is used to describe a broad range of adverse childhood experiences that can be stressful or traumatic events that children and young people can be exposed to.

My view is that we should also be considering AAE's (Adverse Adult Experiences) too, after all, we did not stop being human at age 18, or affected by adversity. By 18 many of us had become parents. Perhaps that research and science is in the future. Did I just invent a new acronym?

ACEs range from experiences that directly harm a child, such as physical, verbal or sexual abuse, and physical or emotional neglect, to those that affect the environments in which children grow up, such as parental separation, domestic violence, mental illness, alcohol abuse, drug use or imprisonment.

Or as I call it; 'the shit that misses the fan and hits you as a kid.'

Childhood experiences, which we all have, both positive and negative, have a massive impact on our lifelong physical and mental health and opportunities.

As such, early experiences are an important public health issue. Much of the foundational research in this area has been referred to as Adverse Childhood Experiences (ACEs).

Adverse Childhood Experiences have been linked to risky health behaviours, chronic health conditions, low life potential, and early death.

As the number of a person's ACEs increases, surprise! - so does the risk for these outcomes. Risk levels are only tempered with the love and support of a constant and genuine care giver if you are lucky enough to have one in your young life.

The wide-ranging health and social consequences of ACEs make clear the importance of preventing them before they happen. The CDC, the guys responsible for conducting the CDC-Kaiser Permanente Adverse Childhood Experiences (ACE) Study, promote lifelong health and well-being through services such as Essentials for Childhood – a framework to assure safe, stable, nurturing relationships and environments for all children. Essentials for Childhood can have a positive impact on a broad range of health problems and on the development of skills that will help children reach their full potential.

It's not Rocket Science but it is science.

My grandmother used to quote 'What you put in is what you get out'.

So, what is the ACEs science if it's not Rocket Science?

ACEs science refers to the research on the prevalence and consequences of adverse childhood experiences, and what to do to prevent them. It comprises:

• The CDC-Kaiser Permanente ACE Study and subsequent surveys that show that most people have at least one ACE, and that people with four ACEs, including living with an alcoholic parent, racism, bullying, witnessing violence outside the home, physical abuse, and losing a parent to divorce — have a huge risk of adult onset of chronic health problems such as heart disease, cancer, diabetes, and alcoholism, and risk of suicide.

• Brain science (neurobiology of toxic stress) — how toxic stress caused by ACEs damages the function and structure of children's developing brains.

• Health consequences — how toxic stress caused by ACEs affects short and long-term health, and can impact every part of the body, leading to autoimmune diseases such as arthritis, as well as heart disease, breast cancer, lung cancer, etc.

• Historical and generational trauma (epigenetic consequences of toxic stress) — how toxic stress caused by ACEs can alter how our DNA functions, and how that can be passed on from generation to generation.

• Resilience research and practice — Building on the knowledge that the brain is plastic and the body wants to heal. This part of ACEs science includes evidence-based practice, as well as practice-based evidence by people, organizations and communities that are integrating trauma-informed and resilience-building practices. This ranges from looking at how the brain of a teen with a high ACE score can be healed with cognitive behaviour therapy, to how schools can integrate trauma-informed and resilience-building practices that result in an increase in students' scores, test grades and graduation rates.

What are ACEs? – run that by me again.

ACEs are adverse childhood experiences that harm a child's developing brain and lead to changing the way they respond to stress and damages their immune system so profoundly that the effects show up decades later. ACEs cause much of our burden of chronic disease, most mental illness, and are at the root of most violence.

"ACEs" comes from the CDC-Kaiser Adverse Childhood Experiences Study, a ground-breaking public health study that discovered that childhood trauma leads to the adult onset of chronic diseases, depression and other mental illness, violence and being a victim of violence, as well as financial and social problems.

The 10 ACEs that the researchers measured:

• Physical, sexual and verbal abuse.
• Physical and emotional neglect.
• A family member who is:
   o depressed or diagnosed with other mental illness;

o   addicted to alcohol or another substance;
o   in prison.
- Witnessing a mother being abused.
- Losing a parent to separation, divorce or other reason.

Since the original ACE Study subsequent ACE surveys have augmented the range of ACEs types to assess various additional experiences such as witnessing a sibling being abused, witnessing violence outside the home, witnessing a father being abused by a mother, being bullied by a peer or adult, involvement with the foster care system, living in a war zone, living in an unsafe neighbourhood, losing a family member to deportation etc.

I had wanted to entitle this book '50 Shades of ACEs' because I could see at least 10 'shades' of similar ACEs between each of the 10 included in the original study.

My personal view and observation is that it is almost irrelevant which ACEs you may list for yourself and score as a 1. What really matters is that we understand that all ACEs, in any shade you endure, have the power to negatively affect your mental and physical health and well-being. 'What you put in is what you get out'

Good in = good out, bad in = bad out, it really is that simple.

So, ACEs, now you understand the annoying American acronym. Love it or hate it, I think we all need to embrace it. It's a great 'brand', people remember it and it starts the conversation, usually with the question 'What are ACEs?'

3. The ACEs Study

No book or conversation on ACEs can skip past the facts produced by the original ACEs study. It is the original study that brings the undeniable truth out of the shadows. It is a truth that has been festering for years in the darkest shadows of modern life.

I personally don't think the science of ACEs is anything new. It is just that we have now been exposed to the brand name 'ACEs', which is a brilliant tag, and the research has been collected and collated and presented graphically in an easily understood and logical way.

I sat and explained it to my 14-year-old daughter and she got it straight away and gave me immediate examples of how ACEs have been affecting the lives of some of her friends. Today's kids are brighter than us, even if they do stupid stuff.

It appears that the 'ordinary' people, the general population, comprehend the bigger picture of ACEs without much persuasion or confusion, whereas, many examples can be found of the science being discarded by some of the intellectual types. Some of whom don't understand that a staple food prepared from a dough of flour and water, usually by baking, often leavened by processes such as reliance on naturally occurring sourdough microbes, chemicals, industrially produced yeast, or high-pressure aeration, is better known by the masses simply as Bread!

As I am writing this I have just had a news item pop up on my PC with the headline 'Scotland embraces ACEs science and trauma-informed approaches' the article, published on the ACEs Connection website, goes on to report;

'It usually takes the passage of time to identify the point when a movement gains momentum and advances to the next level. Reflecting on the evolution of Scotland's ACEs/trauma-informed movement, one of its early leaders, Dr. Michael Smith, says the foundation was just being built two years ago when a catalytic visit by Jane Stevens, founder and publisher of ACEs Connection, galvanized core activists and convinced naysayers that ACEs science was real and had the power to transform lives and systems across society.

Stevens' talks two years ago turned some sceptics around and provided inspiration to believers just at the right time, according to Smith who invited her to Scotland after he heard her speak several months before in New York City.

Some of the key milestones and activities include two reports that set priorities for Scotland, dozens of screenings of the film Resilience followed by panel discussions, the formation of a national ACEs HUB to enhance information sharing, and the creation of dedicated staff positions within the Scotland government to address ACEs.'

I am hoping we can replicate this in Cumbria.

It appears that the sceptical dismissal by the naysayers is turning into a more positive mantra and 'sliced bread is no longer important.'

I am working with THE CUMBRIA RESILIENCE PROJECT group here in the UK and we have attracted more than 240 people to our recently published ACEs forum.

In the last 24 hrs. I have had 367 email enquiries for accredited ACEs training that is being put together for release later in the year. It appears that even some of the stiff upper lipped English naysayers are jumping on board with us ordinary folk.

I have had hundreds of social media comments, emails, text messages, and telephone calls from Doctors, Teachers, Healthcare workers, Social workers, Residential childcare workers, Psychologists, Police staff and, perhaps more importantly, but sadly, many, many survivors with high scores of ACEs.

All with a hunger to understand and promote awareness of ACEs and ACEs science.

So, let's look at the highlights of the research. All the data is available for minute scrutiny if you have the time. The original ACEs Study has published about 70 research papers since 1998. Hundreds of additional research papers based on the ACEs Study have also been published. My own 'ACEs research' search on Google today delivered almost 15 million results in 0.42 seconds. I guess my contribution (this book) may take it to 15 million and 1 at some point.

The original USA ACEs study found that around two thirds (64%) of the 17,000 individuals included in the study reported at least one ACE, with over a quarter (26%) having suffered physical abuse, and a fifth experiencing some form of sexual abuse. Around one in eight individuals (13%) had experienced four or more ACEs

More recent studies here in the UK, in the Midlands area for example, found that almost half (47%) of that adult population (aged 18-69 years) had at least 1 ACE, with many people having higher ACE scores. 53% had experienced 0 ACEs, 19% had experienced 1 ACE, 16% had experienced 2-3 ACEs, and 12% had experienced 4+ ACEs.

The same study confirmed previous evidence that there is a strong dose-response relationship between ACEs and poor physical and mental health, chronic disease (such as type II diabetes, chronic obstructive pulmonary disease; heart disease and cancer), increased levels of violence, and lower academic success both in childhood and adulthood.

I did my own unofficial and simple ACEs research analysis. I scrutinised an old black and white photograph of mine.

Taken in 1969 The photograph shows many young boys aged 6 – 15 who were all abandoned in a notoriously bad children's home that was owned by a predatory paedophile who is now serving several concurrent life sentences for CSA crimes. (Child Sexual Abuse)

Based on what I know about those of us in the picture who have not committed suicide or died from substance misuse and other health-related problems, I know without any doubt that most of the survivors from that picture have lived their lives blighted by ACEs.

Collectively, we each had ACEs before we were placed in residential care and we all left with more to add to the score.

Here is a list of known outcomes for the boys who survived who I know personally.
Denial, disbelief, confusion, difficulty concentrating, anger, irritability, mood swings, anxiety, fear, guilt, shame, self-blame, withdrawing from others, feeling sad, feeling hopeless, feeling disconnected, depression, dissociation, impaired relationships, low self-esteem, sexual dysfunction, sleep disturbance, suicidal ideas and behaviour, alcoholism and alcohol abuse, chronic obstructive pulmonary disease, depression, poor health-related quality of life, Illicit drug use, ischemic heart disease, liver disease, poor work performance, financial stress, multiple sexual partners, smoking, unintended pregnancies, early initiation of

smoking, early initiation of sexual activity, poor academic achievement.

One photograph, one group of children, one time and place with multiple ACEs; reaching from then to now (49 years) like an insidious vein that continues to bleed through blighted lives, with ACEs in the shadows.

A 2012 epidemiological study revealed that there was increased risk (adjusted odds ratio) of having health and social problems in adulthood for those individuals who had experienced 4+ ACEs, compared to those with no ACEs.

The statistics are shocking and show unequivocally that individuals with 4 or more ACEs were:

- 4.5 times more likely to have become pregnant or got somebody pregnant under 18 years of age
- 30.6 times more likely to have had a sexually transmitted infection (STI)
- 1.8 times more likely to be morbidly obese
- 2.3 times more likely to have liver or digestive disease
- 1.5 times more likely to have stayed overnight in hospital in the last 12 months
- 3.7 times more likely to a regular heavy drinker
- 3.9 times more likely to be a current smoker
- 9.7 times more likely to be a heroin or crack user
- 5.2 times more likely to have been hit in the last 12 months
- 7.9 times more likely to have hit someone in the last 12 months
- 8.8 times more likely to have been in prison or cells

These figures were like the English ACEs population study which found, across England, 53% had experienced 0 ACEs, 23% had experienced 1 ACE, 15% had experienced 2-3 ACEs and 9% had experienced 4+ ACEs.

Findings from a national study across Wales found adults who had suffered four or more types of ACEs were almost 10 times more likely to have felt suicidal or self-harmed than those who had experienced none.

Results from the first Welsh Adverse Childhood Experiences study also show that suffering four or more harmful experiences in childhood increases the chances of high-risk drinking in adulthood by four times, being a smoker by six times and being involved in violence in the last year by around 14 times.

The same Welsh survey revealed around one in every seven adults aged 18-69 years in Wales had experienced four or more Adverse Childhood Experiences during their childhood and just under half had each experienced at least one ACE they could identify.

In Scotland the government have published various official statements supporting the research and the now proven science of ACEs.

All the studies referred to can be found on the internet, They say that childhood adversity can create harmful levels of stress which impact healthy brain development that can result in long-term effects on learning, behaviour and health and they confirm that the evidence from ACEs surveys, in the US, UK and elsewhere, demonstrated that ACEs can exert a significant influence throughout a person's life.

ACEs have been found to be associated with a range of poorer health and social outcomes in adulthood and that these risks increase and the higher the ACEs score, the higher the risk for these outcomes.

Scotland is amid a cultural revolution. They have the aim of getting the information on Adverse Childhood Experiences (ACEs) to every citizen across the 5 million of that diverse nation. Their goal is to make SCOTLAND the World's First ACEs-aware nation.

I took the vision with a smaller goal to make Cumbria England's first ACEs aware region. We are 500,000 citizens spread across a huge geographical footprint and with a fair share of naysayers rooted in healthcare. Thank any god you wish for the determination of the grass-roots ACEs movement now emerging here in Cumbria.

In the last 40 days, 16 free screenings of the film RESILIENCE have been organised.

I have also been invited to become a Director and Board member of the newly formed England North: ACEs Network.

The group has a vision to lead on solutions with a clear mission statement; The opportunity to build on lessons already learned, together with the willingness of organisations and agencies to work more collaboratively, leads to the possibility of a trauma-informed movement of front-line practitioners working together on Public Health Solutions to reducing adversity in childhood experiences.

The group includes:

- Dr Wendy Thorley PhD, M.Ed., B.A (Hons) Ed. R.G.N. National Teaching Fellow HEA. Director of CEL&T. Co-Founder ACE Network North East. Director of New Blueprint Group.
- Nick Mason OBE. Lambeth Safer Neighbourhood Board (LSNB) Chair, Cumbria Police Engagement Lead,
- Rachel Lofthouse, Professor of Teacher Education in the Carnegie School of Education.
- Jane Pickthall, North Tyneside Virtual School Head.
- Al Coats MBE, Independent Social Worker, Member DfE Expert Advisory Group on Adoption Support, Director CEL&T.
- Alastair Reid, LSNB Programme Manager, Community Engagement Manager

...and me with my 10 ACEs and a knobbly-knees certificate from Butlins Holiday Camp Circa 1965.

So, moving on, I don't know about you, but I am convinced.

The more sceptical of you should do your own research and reach your own conclusions.

I say ACEs are real and ACEs are linked to a wide range of negative physical and mental health outcomes.

The chapter entitled: How ACEs affected my life, will provide you with hard hitting real-life evidence provided by me and confirmed by an eminent Professor of Psychiatry who produced a 32-page report about me with a prognosis that confirms a link between my own ACEs and health outcomes, which he says I am: 'Unlikely to ever make a complete recovery from'.

4.   The ACEs Movement

Before we get to the more personal chapters of this book, I want to briefly bring your attention to the phenomenal growth of what has been called the ACEs Movement, formed by the people rooted in the grass across the USA and the UK who have been shaking some medical and social service establishments out of their complacent nests upon high.

In fact, I will include YOU as part of this movement, if you have fire in your belly for spreading the knowledge about ACEs, and like me you have had that light-bulb moment when you first listened to Dr Nadine Burke-Harris explaining the bear in the forest and the trip to the well to see what the hell was in it.

The Adverse Childhood Experiences (ACEs) Movement consists of hundreds of grassroots initiatives that have emerged across America, UK, and around the World.

Each part of the movement is developing creative interventions and "tests of change" in a wide variety of imaginative ways, not all on the same paragraph, but all on the same page, and each group is driven passionately to reduce the incidence and societal effects of Adverse Childhood Experiences and to promote healing from these experiences. The movement is responding to the ACEs study science at a rapid pace.

Dr. Robert Anda calls ACEs "chronic" and "insidious," rolling out from generation to generation via epigenetic inheritance. This statement should be all that is needed to get our serious attention and move us into to action.

The ACEs Movement is raging like rapid fire from an inferno, rising out of the need for a multidirectional all-inclusive community effort to create a public health change which is being instigated by individuals, institutions and government systems that are too often operating in a different library, let alone on different pages of the same book.

The general population, everyone, (You and me) are essential to the process of change, it's a grass-roots movement, from bottom up.

The institutions and government systems engagement in ACEs science is still essential though, because without structure and appropriate support services in place to surround individuals who become ACEs aware, the revolutionary knowledge that is intended to help people, could have the potential to perpetuate the cycle of trauma and possibly make things worse.

Like the workings of an 18th century fob watch, every cog, minutest and large, has an important role to play. I can hear younger people asking, 'what's a fob watch?' Let's hope in years to come young people will be equally puzzled when you tell them there was a time when the understanding of ACEs science did not exist. For me, it is Dr Nadine Burke Harris who is my modern-day Florence Nightingale.

"I think one's feelings waste themselves in words; they ought all to be distilled into actions which bring results" Florence Nightingale

Known as 'The Lady with the Lamp", Florence Nightingale famously nursed wounded soldiers during the Crimean War. Her dedication altered public perception of the profession and her insistence on sanitary conditions for patients is believed to have saved many lives. In other words, she ignited a radical yet simple paradigm shift with her peers.

Dr Nadine Burke Harris, another lady holding a lamp and instigating an equally radical paradigm shift, was two years into her ACEs journey when her ACEs TEDMED talk was recorded. She was the Centre for Youth Wellness Founder and CEO and, in my opinion, the emerging face of ACEs awareness around the World.

That 16 minutes of wisdom has now been viewed 3 million+ times. When I first listened to her talk my understanding and my life changed. That TEDMED talk has been pivotal as an international message of ACEs and toxic stress awareness.

It was the bear in the forest that resonated with my soul on that day.

"...imagine you're walking in the forest and you see a bear. Immediately, your hypothalamus sends a signal to your pituitary, which sends a signal to your adrenal gland that says, "Release stress hormones! Adrenaline! Cortisol!" And so, your heart starts to pound, your pupils dilate, your airways open up, and you are ready to either fight that bear or run from the bear. And that is wonderful if you're in a forest and there's a bear. But the problem is what happens when the bear comes home every night, and this system is activated over and over and over again, and it goes from being adaptive, or life-saving, to maladaptive, or health-damaging. Children are especially sensitive to this repeated stress activation, because their brains and bodies are just developing. High doses of adversity not only affect brain structure and function, they affect the developing immune system, developing hormonal systems, and even the way our DNA is read and transcribed." Dr Nadine Burke Harris

After adding up the number of forests I had been in as a child, and the number of attacking bears I had encountered, I was literally stunned into silent contemplation, frozen in a sense of shock while the reality of my own ACEs in the shadows came into focus for the first time in my life.

I watched the TEDMED talk a dozen times that day, hanging on every word.

As the science and research of ACEs was explained by Dr Burke-Harris I had a light-bulb moment, realising I scored 10 on the original ACEs questionnaire. Everything that Dr Nadine Burke Harris said brought understanding and an overwhelming feeling of relief.

I felt like I had finally found something that made some sense of my life journey and since that day I have been determined to spread the word and knowledge about ACEs.

I am a preacher of ACEs truth, a silent evangelist seeking to proselytize at every opportunity in my own stealthy way. Or, more accurately, I am a 'Gobby Scouser' with little education and all fired up in my belly with a fervent focus to incite change. "...and if they don't like it they can just f**k off."
Don't be offended, I am just making my point with a little tongue in cheek scouse humour.

The Centre of Youth Wellness in the USA, led by Dr Nadine Burke Harris as CEO, stands at the forefront of an ACEs movement being driven by paediatric clinicians, educators, parents, policymakers and other child-serving professionals and advocates who are working together to implement universal screening for Adverse Childhood Experiences (ACEs), and treat the effects of toxic stress.

In the UK, ACEs forums, health care groups, government officials, practitioners from all sectors, and numerous other individuals, are following the lead of the trailblazers in USA and catching on to the ACEs Movement vision.

This little book is one of the three things I am doing (from my garden office) to play my active part in the ACEs movement and, hopefully, bringing another voice to the choir. It may be out of tune but it's the only voice I have.

What will you be doing?

5. How I Score 10 ACEs

This is not an autobiography, so I will refrain from giving you 'my story' in that frame. However, the most valuable experience I can draw from is my own life, so I will have to give you my answers from the ACEs questionnaire to explain them.

Breaking off from this explanation of how I score 10 ACEs for a moment, I want to relay something to you that happened yesterday as I first sat at my desk to start this chapter.

I took a cup of tea to my wife who was in bed. I found her sobbing her heart out and with a look of fear and total bewilderment on her face. I immediately comforted her and asked her what was wrong.

Thing is, she did not know who I was, she did not know where she was, and the look of terror in her face increased when she was unable to name our children, her mother's name, or the name of the cat who had jumped on the bed.

It took a good hour to console and reassure her. This had never happened before. She's younger than me at 52 and scores lower on the ACEs questionnaire.

After seeing 2 doctors, having a CT scan, some blood tests, and waiting 7 hours in hospital, the diagnosis came back as TGA - Transient Global Amnesia 'probably' caused by stress at work, but also with a slim chance of it being part of a mini-stroke.

She's home now and functioning as normal but fatigued.

My wife works in children's services and at the challenging end of lives so obviously messed up by generational ACEs. In addition, she has been absorbing me and my 10 ACEs for 30 years (give that woman a medal) on top of our own challenges of raising 6 children together and losing a daughter to stillbirth.

So, I am not surprised that she had a global meltdown, albeit thankfully only for a short time.

The underlying cause of transient global amnesia is unknown. There appears to be a link between transient global amnesia and a history of migraines, though the underlying factors that contribute to both conditions aren't fully understood. Commonly reported events that may trigger transient global amnesia include acute emotional distress, as might be provoked by bad news, conflict or overwork. This past week we both endured an event of acute emotional stress.

Why I am telling you this?

Well, apart from what happened to my wife, I was also challenged yesterday during the hours that we sat in the A&E department observing the lives of those arriving and those being discharged.

I found myself mentally counting the obvious ACEs in the lives of people around me. Some talking to each other about their lives and how they ended up in A&E, and others sitting silently and yet I could 'see' the ACEs outcomes.

We witnessed a distressed dad carrying a toddler with a 14 year old boy by his side and we shuddered as we heard the dad tell the receptionist in an agitated manner "he's swallowed a penny, and he's been sick, and he's drowsy" then adding "I left him for a few minutes with his brother (the young boy standing next to him) and I expected him to keep him safe" adding a loud tut and a look of stern disapproval directed at the boy.

I felt like dragging the idiot father out of A&E to give him a lesson about ACEs and how he was burdening his poor young son with guilt that was not his. Then I remembered that there was a time when I had done similar things.

Before I was ACEs aware.

I watched that young lad as he sank into to depths of guilt and worry with the burden of blame that had been placed publicly on his young shoulders by his dad. Yep, I thought to myself, that is an adverse childhood experience right there. I wonder how many more he has at home.

We then watched a very frail women, not old, but so worn down with obvious alcoholism that she looked like 70 when she was probably mid-forties. As she slowly dragged her feet around the waiting room, with her soiled jeans halfway down her legs and gasping for breath and with her hunched over stature, no one took much notice; apart from casting looks of disapproval and moving away from her.

We subsequently observed a young man arrive to support her. It was her son, aged around 20-25. He spent several hours pacing the room, up and down. A face full of worries, embarrassed, avoiding eye contact and perplexed by his mother's situation.

When he did sit down he was slouched with his head in his hands staring aimlessly at the floor where, no doubt he could see the abyss of his mother's life, past and present, fuelled and destroyed with alcohol abuse. I wonder how many ACEs are in that family's story?

In came a very elderly frail old man in a wheelchair, maybe in his late 90's and probably a young veteran of World War II. He had cuts and bruises all over his arms and head. Had he fallen? Or was he pushed? Who knows? Who cares?

He was left by the staff and told the taxi would take him home. He looked frightened, bewildered, and had the same expression on his face my wife had that morning when she did not know who she was or where she was. One hour later, with no support or reassurance, the overweight disgruntled taxi driver collected him and his newly acquired walking frames and whisked him away. Neither of them made eye contact with each other or with anyone in the room.

Who was at home for this old guy? Who was going to help him? Why had they not cleaned up the congealed blood on his face, neck and arms?

How many ACEs have these people endured? Later in the day a young man turned up with cuts and bruises and a large bump on the side of his head. He was agitated, unkempt, and had an angry look. I somehow knew by his demeanour he had seen the inside of a prison cell.

As the day unfolded, simply by observing and listening, we learned that this young lad had been attacked by five youths after they had stopped him outside a shop and had taken his sunglasses by force from his head saying it was a 'tax' payment for being in 'their' area of town.

Gangs are on the rise in the UK folks, and yes it was daylight robbery and assault; but no one witnessed anything.

That lad had been in prison for drugs misuse and a collection of other 'minor' crimes since his teenage years. The police arrived and interviewed him publicly, right there in the waiting room. One hour later, we all knew he was a victim of an attack, we knew he was homeless, and we knew he had previously been on an electronic tag. We also knew he had mental health problems, as he said it out loud himself.

That young man's dad turned up and they had a few feisty verbal exchanges. We watched the body language of the dad along with his head shaking and dismissive 'tuts' that he expressed continually, with his arms folded tightly and not daring to look his son in the eye.

I filled in the blanks of their lives and scored them both as 4 or more ACEs – no doubt about it.

I wondered if the first father would be sat here with either of his sons in years to come.

I thought to myself, 'This is a bloody epidemic, what the hell is going on with society?'

This was one A&E, in one hospital, on one sunny afternoon, and just a few people observed.

So, I will leave those observations with you.

Back to how I score 10 ACEs.

Adverse Childhood Experience (ACE) Questionnaire

While you were growing up, during your first 18 years of life:

1. Did a parent or other adult in the household OFTEN:
    - swear at you, insult you, put you down, or humiliate you?
    - Or act in a way that made you afraid that you might be physically hurt?
    - Or did other children, including brothers and sisters, OFTEN hit you, threaten you, pick on you or insult you?

    Yes   or   No   If yes enter 1 [1]

My step father swore at me, insulted me, put me down, and humiliated me. He was violent towards me and my mother and he made me afraid of him. I lived in fear (from aged 5 to 9) that I may be physically hurt by him at any point in any day and for any reason.

When I was placed in a children's home I was bullied for the first 18 months because I was 'perceived' to be a posh kid. I was slapped, prodded, pushed, and punched by older boys. I was named-called and belittled by boys and staff because of my tall and thin stature. They called me Twiggy.

---

2. Did a parent or other adult in the household OFTEN:
    - push, grab, slap, or throw something at you (other than spanking)?
    - Or ever hit you so hard that you had marks or were injured?

    Yes   or   No   If yes enter 1 [1]

When I was 18 months old I was left for three days with a broken collar bone before receiving treatment at the hospital.

My step father pushed me, grabbed me, slapped me, and often threw household items in a rage. My step father poked me in the chest with his finger so hard I was often bruised. My step father force fed me with hot sprouts from a pan while sitting on my chest (he was a big little man and weighed about 15 stone) pushing them one after the other into my mouth because I had refused to eat them. I choked on the sprouts. My step-father hung me by my ankles from a first story window (aged 7) and threatened to drop me.

----

3. Did an adult or person at least 5 years older than you EVER:

• touch or fondle you or have you touch their body in a sexual way?

• Or try to or actually have oral, anal, or vaginal sex with you?

Yes   or   No   If yes enter 1 [1]

When I was in a children's home (aged 12 – 15) I was touched, fondled, masturbated, and repeatedly anally raped over a period of three years by two adults and one older boy.

----

4. Did you OFTEN feel:

• that no one in your family loved you or thought you were important or special?

• Or that your family didn't look out for each other, feel close to each other, or support each other?

• Or lonely, rejected or that nobody liked you?

Yes   or   No   If yes enter 1 [1]

As a very young child my mother often abandoned me. My wider family was dysfunctional and constantly arguing with each other in my presence. I witnessed arguing and violence between my natural parents and my mother and step-fathers. I had no sustained or appropriate support or nurturing from birth to aged 18. I often felt lonely, rejected, and abandoned as a young child, and later while living in a children's home. While attending regular school I felt rejected, disliked, and bullied by teachers, parents, and other children because I was living in a children's home.

----

5.   Did you OFTEN feel that:
    •   you didn't have enough to eat, had to wear dirty clothes, and had no one to protect you?
    •   Or that your parents were too drunk or high to take care of you or take you to the doctor if you needed it?
    •   Or was there a period of 2 years or more where your family was very poor or unable to afford necessities like food and clothes?
Yes   or   No   If yes enter 1 [1]

I was often left alone by my mother and step father, I was hungry. I was occasionally left to wear soiled underwear. I remember being frightened and alone with no reliable adult to depend on. I was left unprotected for long periods of time. My step father was a violent alcoholic. For a period during my childhood I lived with my mother and grandmother who were both at that time alcoholics. Aged 11, I was suffering from depression and several other serious conditions. I visited an A&E department in a children's hospital, alone and frightened, asking for their help.

When my mother separated from her second husband we were escorted by police to protect us both from violence. We subsequently lived in a near derelict house. Food and clothing was scarce, and my bed was a door propped up on wooden crates.

---

6. Was a biological parent EVER lost to you through divorce, abandonment or any other reason?

Yes   or   No   If yes enter 1 [1]

I was separated from my biological father when I was under 18 months old. I was separated from my biological mother when she abandoned me when I was aged 12.

---

7. Was your parent or carer OFTEN:
    • pushed, grabbed, slapped, or had something thrown at him/her?
    • Or SOMETIMES or OFTEN kicked, bitten, hit with a fist, or hit with something hard?
    • Or EVER repeatedly hit over at least a few minutes or threatened with a gun or knife?
    • Or did you live for 2 years or more in a neighbourhood that was dangerous or where you saw people being assaulted?

Yes   or   No   If yes enter 1 [1]

I witnessed my mother being repeatedly threatened and beaten by my step-father. She was slapped, pulled, pushed, scratched, slapped, punched, and kicked. I lived in a children's home (community) that had a brutal and violent regime for more than 3 years. I witnessed high levels of violence between children, teenagers, and staff. I witnessed stabbings and people being hit with snooker balls, snooker cues and other objects. I witnessed children being seriously assaulted by staff.

----

8. Did you live with anyone who was a problem drinker or alcoholic or who used street drugs?

Yes   or   No   If yes enter 1 [1]

My step father, my biological mother, grandmother, and auntie were all alcoholics. One of the adult perpetrators who raped me was an alcoholic. When I absconded from the children's home I lived for short periods with older family members (teenagers) who were using street drugs.

----

9. Was a household member depressed or mentally ill or did a household member attempt suicide?

Yes   or   No   If yes enter 1 [1]

My biological mother, grandmother and aunty suffered from depression. All three had suicidal rumination. One of them did attempt suicide on more than one occasion.

----

10. Did a household member go to prison?

Yes   or   No   If yes enter 1 [1]

My mother told me that my biological father served a prison sentence for non-payment of maintenance. He has confirmed that, on principle, he refused to pay maintenance for both me and my mother, opting to only offer payment for my upkeep.

6.   How ACEs affected my life

I could write reams on this subject, but I will not subject you to that.

What I feel is paramount for me to achieve in this chapter is to clearly demonstrate the link of my childhood 10 ACEs score, that you have just reviewed, directly to the lived experiences and physical/mental health outcomes in my adult years.

If this link is true for me, it may be true for you, and for others.

What I hope is that my real-life example, which is supported with medical evidence, will have more impact than simply reviewing the published statistics of any number of ACEs research.

I know the reality of ACEs first-hand, so for me, it's truly validated beyond any doubt.

So, how did ACEs affect my life?

The list of outcomes, identified in the chapter entitled 'The ACEs study', is a full and complete list.

However, I will touch on the main ACEs outcomes in my life that I believe had the most damaging affect.

In no particular order.

I had my trust button (the natural and much needed ability to trust anyone) damaged so badly that I believe the neurons and synaptic connections in my developing brain had a democratic vote at some point early on in my childhood and decided it was a very bad idea to trust anyone. The little buggers turned the process off and then destroyed it.

Let's stop right there. How bad was that for me? Well, I can tell you that trusting other humans, at any level, is surely an essential part of living a healthy human life. It's one of the basic requirements for our modern day living.

I did not trust children, adults, or even myself and my own instincts. As I got older, age 5, 9, 12, 14,15, it just got worse as the adverse experiences mounted up.

From being a toddler to a man of 50 pus years, I lived in a state of hyper-vigilance, viewing every encounter with human beings as a potential bear in the forest moment that I had to quickly control, fight or flee. An exhausting and all-consuming way to live that has almost broken me on a few occasions.

Yes, I have attempted suicide and I have had regular suicidal thoughts.

I lost all confidence in myself and my abilities.

I have lived my life with low self-esteem and with an overwhelming but hidden fear of dogs and men.

My step father had controlled me with the threat that his dogs would attack me if I misbehaved.

It was a man who raped me and other males who sexually and physical assaulted me.

It was my mother who abandoned me.

Subsequently, I viewed all men as predatory paedophiles and I was convinced that every female I connected with would be disloyal. No one was to be trusted, in any way, ever.

To counter this, I developed a number of complex and very convincing personas that I could pull from the pack at any time to present to the world, depending on the situation I was in at the time. It started as young as 5 when for many months, I pretended I could not talk, and the adults took me to see a child psychologist.

This got me some much-needed attention from caring grownups which I enjoyed while it lasted.

More complex coping mechanisms continued to develop throughout my life as I adopted different lifestyles and personas. Each persona working itself out in different relationships and lifestyles.

The most obvious being through employment which included times working as a builder, graphic designer, trawlerman, businessman, evangelistic preacher, and mental health worker; to name just a few.

My adult life has been lived at one hundred miles an hour and I have unwittingly drawn many people into that very energetic creative vibrant and tumultuous process along the way, both at work and in my private life; which was never private. The faster I lived, the easier it was to ignore my nightmares.

I was unaware of these complex coping mechanisms at the time, but with hindsight and the educated opinion of others, I now understand that I have invented many personas over 61 years. Reinventing myself each time life imploded.

As a child I learned to be all things to all men, so to speak. This early learned strategy for survival developed over time into a complex adult approach to every part of my life.

I had learned the art of manipulation at a very young age. It was the only way that I could survive the chaotic and unstable world that the idiots in charge had created around me.

Attaining love, nurturing, and attention became a complex and carefully considered manoeuvre for me. It occupied most of my head space.

I also became a sex addict; wanting to have sex with every woman you meet is not normal behaviour in any book.

Again, with the benefit of hindsight, it has become obvious to me now. Apart from seeking a 'mother figure' I also needed to prove to myself and others that I was not a 'bummer' (kids-home speak for homosexual - mixed with an obscure view that homosexual meant predatory paedophile). Which of course it does not.

I also desperately yearned for love and affection and meaningful human interaction. That experience, throughout my childhood, had been seriously obscured by the adults I encountered along the way.

It was only as a 'special boy' that I was shown kindness and 'love' and a corrupt version of parental care giving and concern that belongs in any hell of your choice.

Is it any wonder that I ran off with a 27-year-old woman and her children when I was just 17?

I was trying very hard to be a man, husband, and step-father, when I was actually an underdeveloped child with no point of reference or positive role-model to emulate.

I was seriously emotionally disabled with an ACEs induced psychological injury that was hidden in the shadows of my apparently high-functioning and creative mind.

A troubled mind that never rested, night or day, without the secret use of sleeping tablets, copious amounts of alcohol, and increasingly complex approaches to living. At 17 I already had the 10 childhood ACEs hiding in the shadows of my life, and each one was affecting the decisions I made while quickly learning to be an adult.

So, how does that play out in the years that followed?

A synopsis.

I have been married three times and have fathered eight children with three different wives. I have had long-term relationships with two other women who already had a child when I met them. One of them also considerably older than me, like my first wife.

I think I have had adult sex with approximately 40 different people; those who I can remember.

I have had in excess of 25 jobs and I have created more than 16 businesses. Most of these employment situations have ended abruptly following conflict with those in charge or with the statutory bodies who tried to hold me to account for things like business loans, accounts, VAT, tax or tax evasion.

I have destroyed profitable businesses, almost overnight, when business partners have been disloyal to me; as far as I am concerned that is.

I have been a single parent, a weekend dad and a full-time dad. A parent, bad and not so bad, for a total of 44 of my 61 years.

I have lived in 22 different houses as an adult, (following 12 as a child) that's 34 addresses spread over 61 years.

I have the next planned move on the horizon, hopefully the final move and for good reasons.

I have been officially declared bankrupt twice with combined personal debts of £120,000. I was once banned from being a company director, by the Secretary of State, for 12 months following an accumulated business debt in excess of 1.4 million pounds. I arrogantly paid my £1 limited liability to the liquidator and walked away to start another business the very next day.

I have managed to gather a few treasured friends who I trust and value in different ways. Some I would trust with my money, some with my children, and some with my wife, but none with them all, except maybe, possibly, one or maybe two. (You know who you are.)

The only human I have come to fully trust unconditionally is my dear wife who has loved me throughout my pain and the pain I have unintentionally caused her and others to endure. She knows my secrets, my nightmares, my feelings of shame, and my insecurities. Lucky for me she has stuck around long enough to see a glimmer of light in the shadows of my dysfunctional mind.

I do of course now love and trust my children.
My trust button, thanks to neuroplasticity, has been getting rebuilt for a number of years. However, my love button, which was also destroyed early on in my childhood (before I got the chance to learn what love was) is taking a little while longer to function properly.
Don't' get me wrong, I have learned what love is. I have seen it portrayed in the soaps and my wife has demonstrated it to me for 30 years, unconditionally. I also now experience it first hand when my grandchildren run into my arms to give this unlikely old grandad a big hug.

I have been expressing my own versions of love-giving for years, since I was a 17-year-old 'adult'. At first it was called sex, then it was called giving gifts, then it was called the provision of the needs of others, then it was called not abandoning my children; even when I desperately wanted to run like Forest Gump away from the responsibilities, disappointments and rejections that even the children you love can heap upon you.

Aged 21 I was ordered by the courts to pay for five maintenance orders following my first divorce. I had become legally responsible to provide for one adult and four children, two of which were not mine.

All through my childhood love had come with a nasty sting in its tail. By the time I was a young adult I was loving people around me through many shades of grey mist and misconception.

I have a caring nature and that has been fortunate. The bastards in my childhood had at least left me with that button to work with.

It has been an attribute left reasonably intact. It is in me naturally (thanks Grandad Tom) and they could not take it away.

Caring has got me into a lot of trouble over the years, often by caring for the wrong people, and sometimes caring so much I was suffocating the people I cared about, thinking it was demonstrating love.

I care about human beings who are weak or disadvantaged or endangered. I care about justice. I care about people, particularly young people, who are vulnerable. Their vulnerability triggers something in me that I find very hard to contain or control.

The problem with my care button has never been as simple as it just being broken or destroyed. It has been doing the job of the trust and love buttons simultaneously, so it has been overworked and misused, mostly by me.

Sometimes I just do not care about anything at all, literally nothing.

I can sometimes wake in the morning to discover that the will to live has left me in the night. I can't explain it here but the 'give a f**k button' simply dies within me, sometimes for a day and sometimes for a week, occasionally longer.

I just function on the care button until it comes back. I am well practiced at hiding all the symptoms of my diagnosed complex post-traumatic stress disorder.

This chapter needs to end before I start blathering on about all sorts of scenarios from my adult life that could clearly demonstrate the link between the ACEs in the shadows of my life and the daily, weekly, monthly, yearly experience of living as a survivor of shit that missed the fan and hit me square in the face many times while growing up.

I will leave you with extracted statements made by an eminent Professor of Psychiatry, who has recently assessed me, on behalf of my lawyers who are trying their best to attain financial compensation for me, for the psychological injury caused by some of the idiots in charge of my childhood.

I will not be holding my breath.

'The law is an ass' According to Mr. Bumble. Oliver Twist. Charles Dickens 1838.

OPINION

"Mr. Survivor is currently suffering with complex Post-Traumatic Stress Disorder of a relatively severe and very chronic nature...he also suffers with a recurrent depressive disorder which is longstanding and, has at times, been severe...the current presentation would suggest a moderately severe depressive episode...his low mood, poor sleep, anxiety, symptoms of panic, disturbed appetite are suggestive of depression and his GP records (covering 55 years) are littered with references to stress-related illness, depression and recurrent depression...there have been profound effects on his personality and his disordered relationship with alcohol and any secondary effect on his physical health are undoubtedly also related to the abuse he has suffered...I note that Mr Survivor is a vulnerable individual constitutionally in terms of the adverse events (ACEs) that he suffered prior to his being placed in (care) and subsequently being subject to protracted sexual abuse and a hostile, unsupportive regime...the admission to care might have been an opportunity to redress some of these issues and provide a stable background but it appears to have been anything but and he was clearly subject to a campaign of sexual abuse, violence and emotional under-support that lasted at least several years...these are the main triggering events (ACEs) for his damaged personality, PTSD and recurrent depression... contributory to his lowered self-esteem and recurrent depression. "

TREATMENT

"...continue his current anti-depressants...may require a mood stabiliser such as Lamotrigine to help prevent further abnormal variation in moods...may benefit from vagal nerve stimulator...medical treatment (required) over the next 4 or 5 years."

PROGNOSSIS

"unfortunately, having suffered protracted episodes of depression and PTSD (he) is likely to be subject to further episodes if he suffers further adverse life events or traumatic events...I do not believe however that he is likely to make a complete or rapid recovery because of the duration of his symptoms since childhood."
Eminent Professor of Psychiatry.

7.   How I am recovering from ACEs

Over the past few months I have been busy raising funds and attracting support for what I have named THE CUMBRIA RESILIENCE PROJECT. This came about after I had read that Scotland had become very forward thinking about ACEs and were stating their intention to become the first ACEs aware nation in the World.

They had started to screen the RESILIENCE film to a wide audience at a grass-roots level and it has gained quick traction and interest since early 2017.

The RESILIENCE film, The Biology of Stress and the Science of Hope, directed by James Redford, the son of the Hollywood actor Robert Redford, chronicles the birth of a new movement among paediatricians, therapists, educators and communities, who are using cutting-edge brain science to raise awareness of ACEs and Toxic Stress.

My thought was; 'I could help make Cumbria England's first ACEs aware region…maybe'

My goal quickly developed to:

- Raise Funds to buy a RESILIENCE FILM licence
- Raise Funds towards the cost of showing the RESILIENCE film for free
- Show the RESILIENCE film to as many people as possible over 2 years
- Publish Adverse Childhood Experiences website
- Set up an ACEs Cumbria social media forum group
- Set up a RESILIENCE PROJECT volunteer group
- Create, publish and provide accredited ACEs training
- Write, promote, and sell a book: 50 Shades of ACEs - ACEs in the shadows

Since attaching that 'to do' list to my fridge at home the past few months have been hectic and very rewarding and also encouraging. I had an idea and it seems to have taken off.

I told people I had the tail of a tiger, only to discover it was a herd of elephants.

You are one of the elephants; I hope.

"Wind back a bit lad, how are you recovering from ACEs?" I hear you ask.

Well, it was realising that I was actually feeling more positive and more energised in a new way, more than ever before, that led me to make the decision to pick up the gauntlet set down by Dr Nadine Burke Harris in her TEDMED TALK.

I have been watching that 16 minutes of wisdom over and over again for a few years and I had recently read her book The Deepest Well which was really inspiring. I decided to join the ACEs movement, and if anyone did not like it they could just 'f**k off'. My voice has a place in the queue whether people like it not.

The whole process has been cathartic for me, writing and talking about my experiences with new people I have met.

Working with a new found focus and purpose also releases strong positive emotions, simply by engaging with like-minded people has helped me to feel better.

The recent journey that brought me to the decision to do 'something' probably started around 2011/2012 when, during one of my annual melt-downs, my wife collapsed in tears in front of me, distraught and telling me that she simply could not carry on any longer.

She went on to explain how frustrated and helpless she had felt for many years as each year my annual meltdown (which I was unaware of) repeatedly hit me, her, and the family; "like a giant steam train crashing into our lives" as she described it, year on year on year. It was not the first time I witnessed her frustration with my complex range of behaviours, but I think it was the first time I truly understood the damage and distress she was describing; and that I was the cause.

It was not unusual for me to just close down for no apparent reason. In the room, but not in the room so to speak. Ignoring everyone and everything as I simply went through the motions of breathing and staring into space for long periods.

Ready to verbally pounce on anyone who, in my mind, was being disloyal, dishonest or not attentive to the cost of living or any number of other obscure issues that I was internally discussing with myself in silence and expecting everyone around me to somehow know what was troubling me.

It was her steam train that hit me hard that day.

I made a promise to her that I would get some help.

I reluctantly asked the GP to refer me to mental health services for some support.

As soon as I mentioned sexual abuse in the same sentence as suicide and Jimmy Saville I had the doctors full and immediate attention.

I was not a victim of Jimmy Saville but following his death, and the exposure of his horrendous litany of sexual crimes against children and vulnerable adults and following a previous 13 million-pound North Wales tribunal, some years earlier (which I consider a 'cover up') sexual abuse of children was back in all the headlines.

The first North Wales child abuse scandal was the subject of a three-year investigation into the physical and sexual abuse of children in care homes in North Wales.

The report into the scandal, headed by retired High Court judge Sir Ronald Waterhouse QC, which was published in 2000, resulted in changes in policy in England and Wales for how authorities deal with children in care.

Following that, in November 2012, new allegations had led to the Prime Minister, David Cameron, announcing that a senior independent figure, later named as Mrs Justice Julia Macur, would examine the conduct and remit of the Waterhouse Inquiry. In addition, the Home Secretary, Theresa May, announced a new police inquiry into how the original allegations were dealt with, as well as an investigation of any new allegations.

The report of phase one of the police investigation, Operation Pallial, was published on 29 April 2013. It set out a total of 140 allegations of abuse at 18 children's homes in North Wales between 1963 and 1992. The police stated in November 2013 that, in the previous year, over 200 people had come forward to assist their enquiries.

In November 2014, the owner of several children's residential homes in the Wrexham area, John Allen, was convicted at Mold Crown Court on 33 counts of sexual abuse against 19 boys and one girl, aged between 7 and 15, during the 1960s and 1970s, and he was sentenced to life imprisonment.

Five of his offences were against me; one carried a life sentence and the other 4 carried 10 years' imprisonment concurrent for each. Two further offences have been left on file with the NCA. (National Crime Agency)

The Government had now leaped into more meaningful action with a second-round of investigations prompted by the revelations about Saville and the apparent Government involvement in rings of paedophiles stretching from London to North Wales and elsewhere.

On the back of that general public awareness, I did not have to work hard to get the GP's attention or the offer of council funding for support from the mental health team and others.

Jim had truly fixed it for me!

I subsequently received medication and good counselling from a variety of services. This included EMDR (Eye Movement Desensitization and Reprocessing) and TF-CBT (Trauma focused cognitive behavioural therapy). I was lucky to be able to see a private clinical psychologist who specialised in complex post-traumatic stress disorder.

A big thank you to Vicky Hastings, Clinical Psychologist, Psychotherapist.

During this same period, I also had UTD (Unstructured Therapeutic Disclosure) support from a well-known charity who devised the brilliant UTD model.

With this invaluable combined support, I became confident enough to go back to the police and report again all the crimes that had been committed against me as a child.

I started sharing some of the deeper more difficult memories that had been haunting me for years. Including the hard fact that I had been raped by an adult when I was a child. They called it buggery in those days, but it was anal rape in any language and I had never previously told anyone, including my wife.
I had reported the other range of abuse crimes before but with no positive results.

Long story short, I spent most of 2012 to 2016, receiving GP support, Mental health team support, Police support, Victim support, and a ton of family support while I was also encountering the very challenging processes of giving hours and hours of witness statements, attending Crown Court and being cross examined by a defence lawyer, and receiving countless hours of ongoing therapy.

Not to mention the intrusive and unwanted media attention.

Simultaneously I was quickly and probably obsessively educating myself.

I read a number of books that collectively helped me understand the effects of what had happened to me as a child, how ACEs had affected my brain, and how I could still bring positive changes to my life.

The book list included:

- Childhood Disrupted, How Your Biography Becomes Your Biology And How You Can Heal by Donna Jackson Nakazawa
- The Chimp Paradox by Prof Steve Peters
- The Devil's Advocate - Child abuse and the men in black by Graham Wilmer MBE.
- Books by Ruby Wax such as; Frazzled and Sane New World
- Instrumental - A memoir of madness, medication and music by James Rhodes
- Supersurvivors – The surprising link between suffering and success by Feldman and Kravetz and perhaps the most important book of all (for me):

- Understanding and treating the life-long consequences of Childhood Sexual Abuse, also by Graham Wilmer MBE and his colleagues Tietavainen, Williams and Joynson.

I also read endless internet documents, blogs, and news items relating specifically to childhood abuse, adverse childhood experiences, brain development and neuroplasticity.

I have no doubt regurgitated much of their wisdom and knowledge in this book.

I also spent most of 2017 studying and completing every relevant course I could get my hands on.

I did a mindfulness diploma and I completed 15 courses made available by the local safeguarding children's board through Barnardo's who I was volunteering with, and I also had valuable Child Protection and Safeguarding - Designated Officer training, which was kindly provided by Joanne Caffrey from TotalTrain.

Over this same period, I managed to successfully claim Criminal Injuries Compensation. This was helpful, money always is, but at the same time it left me feeling like the CICA (Criminal Injuries Compensation Authority) did not appreciate the real damage that was caused by the abuse.

Their matter of fact approach was dismissive in nature and I had to almost beg and plead for the legally due payment, which in the end, was low and incorrect.

I believe they took advantage of my lack of knowledge and my poor mental state at the time and under paid me by a considerable amount. I have appealed, and they have repeatedly dismissed my letters.

A lawyer is now making an appeal on my behalf.

I have also convinced a specialist lawyer and barrister to represent me in my attempt to attain compensation from the council's social service department who, in my opinion, dumped me in an unregulated children's home and left me there without any real concern for my well-being.

What has this got to do with my recovery from ACEs?

Everything.

For me, there is no single medication, therapeutic process, or gem of wisdom from any book, that I could single out as the definitive cause of my ongoing sustainable recovery from ACEs.

I can say that the most important thing to me has been my wife's unconditional love, followed by the acceptance of who I am by my children, despite me letting them down on more than one occasion.

Unconditional love is the most powerful tool in the box. The daily practice of mindfulness also comes to mind as being particularly significant for me and my sustainable recovery process.

Being believed in a Crown Court and getting subsequent justice has played a huge part in the process of recovery, (this is not for everyone I know) as has the process of learning how the brain develops and how adverse childhood experiences have been at the root of my adult behaviours and mistakes.

ACEs are not a convenient excuse for my reckless adult life and behaviours, but they go a long way in explaining how they are connected.

'What you put in is what you get out.'

I feel like I am now slowly re-emerging as the good, loving, caring, and productive creative person I was meant to be; before the idiots in charge interrupted my childhood with their abuses of parental and care providing responsibilities that left me physically and psychologically damaged.

ACEs are no longer defining my future and ACEs are not my destiny.

How am I sustainably recovering from ACEs?

Love, education, medication, therapy, time, justice and more love.

Did I mention love?

If you are supporting someone with ACEs, start with love.

Love has the power to conquer anything that is lurking in the darkest of shadows of any life blighted by adverse childhood experiences.

8.   What can YOU do about ACEs?

When I set out to write this short book (or is it a booklet?) I knew generally what I wanted to get across to you, but I had no idea how it would unfold. I just sat in front of my PC and started typing what came to mind. Fortunately, others have helped me with grammar and spelling and have offered suggestions along the way.
I did feel that the last chapter, this one, would perhaps be the most important one.

I have noticed that most people, having read about or listened to the whole ACEs science conversation, or have watched the RESSILIENCE film, immediately ask the question "How do I help people with ACEs?" or "What can I do about ACEs?"

I will break down my own answer to these questions into two parts at the end of the chapter. Firstly, dealing with my view on ACEs prevention and reduction, and secondly my view on ACEs sustainable recovery.

It will be my personal view and it is not intended as an authoritative guide. This book has a simple goal bringing attention to ACEs, but it is not in any way claiming to provide definitive answers, instruction, or guidelines for others to follow.

It's my own blathering about ACEs and is taken from the fog in my own damaged mind. You can decide for yourself what you do with it, that is your responsibility, and not mine.

My views are unqualified, they are simply based on my own interpretation of what I have read, and my first-hand experiences.

For these reasons I have asked three other people to provide their own answers to the chapter question 'What can YOU do about ACEs?'

Al Coates, Judy James, and Laura McConnell are all people who I have met on my recent CUMBRIA RESILIENCE PROJECT journey. They have valuable experience, both academic and lived, and I am truly grateful that they made time at short notice to contribute to this important last chapter.

They are all on the same page with ACEs and ACE awareness and each have their unique and valid voice to add to the ACEs conversation.

Al Coates

Al Coates MBE: is an experienced Social Worker who has extensive knowledge of Fostering, independent Social Work as well as Social Work Practice Educator and Trainer.

As a member of the Department for Education's Expert Advisory Group on Adoption Support (now replaced by Adopter Reference group) he has undertaken to help support families who adopt, recognising these children and young people who are adopted can present with a wide range of challenging behaviours.

As a father of 6 Adopted Children he is well aware of the diverse needs of children who are adopted. In addition, managing his own Foster Care caseload and working with those who Foster as well as those who provide residential settings for children who are Looked After, he understands that children and young people can often display behaviour that can be viewed as unacceptable, aggressive or violent; and managing these behaviours places immense pressure on those within the family setting.

Al runs a popular blogging site at alcoates.co.uk; for which he was awarded First4Adoptions blogger of the year in 2015 and 2016 and also produces the Adoption and Fostering Podcast which is available at: http://adoptionandfostering.podbean.com.

In recognition to his commitment and work he was awarded his MBE in the New Year's Honours list, January 2018.

He has presented at a number of events as a Key Note Speaker and an invited contributor at regional and National conferences and events, discussing Child to Parent Violence or Aggression, following the success of the CPV publications with Dr Wendy Thorley in January 2017.

Judy James

Judy is the founder of Emotion Focus http://www.emotionfocus.co.uk/ - a forward-thinking coaching, training and therapy practice dedicated to seeing people thrive and feel good.

As an experienced coach-therapist, Judy has long been aware that our strongest memories are formed when we experience strong emotions, but it has been a more recent realisation that the body holds the memory of infant and childhood experiences.

Through the diligent practice of Emotion Coaching and Emotion Focused Therapy, Judy works collaboratively with couples and individuals whose early life experiences of adversity, inconsistent care-giving and absence of emotional security show up in later life in the form of physical symptoms, impaired psychological well-being, and in adult relationships.

For businesses and organisations, Judy delivers workshops on the impact of emotion in the workplace in respect of productivity, decision-making, team cohesion, employee wellbeing and motivation.

She also provides training for school and nursery staff to become 'ACE Aware, Attachment Wise and Trauma Informed', so that they can recognise stress behaviours and help children develop emotional literacy and regulation.

Her professional journey into the world of psychotherapy and coaching started almost 30 years ago.

The training and coaching Judy provides has all the theoretical and psychological underpinning you'd expect from an advanced practitioner working with people in relationships; relationships within businesses and teams, in partnerships and families, as well as helping people to develop positive, healthy relationships with themselves.

Laura McConnell

Laura is a teacher, writer and ADHD campaigner from Edinburgh and the main areas of her focus is education and mental health.

Her greatest passion is raising awareness of ADHD. Laura works with a support group, and several UK based ADHD charities, to raise the public profile of ADHD.

Her aim is to highlight the issues surrounding diagnosis and support structures for adults and children with an ADHD diagnosis, contributing to the public narrative surrounding this common neurodevelopmental condition.

Laura is also passionate about increasing access to quality STEM resources (Science, Technology, Engineering and Mathematics)

After completing a professional development course in Outdoor Learning via the outdoor charity, 'Grounds for Learning' in 2013/2014, Laura was awarded Professional Recognition in Outdoor Learning by the General Teaching Council Scotland (GTCS).

Laura's subsequent work with children in the outdoor setting led to an invitation by Usborne to consult on, "The Usborne Outdoor Book" which was published in September 2016.

You can find out more information about her Consultancy work at www.mindsfull.net and further information about Laura's writing at www.lauramcconnell.com.

8a. Al Coates - What can YOU do about ACEs?

Like most people, I find the evidence that is presented through the ACEs study compelling. Having worked and lived in the world of social care for the best part of 20 years the message that early childhood adversity has potentially long term and life limiting implications comes as little surprise.

I can recall during my social work degree I spent three months working in an outreach centre for adults with significant mental ill health. At the end of the very enlightening, challenging and heart rending months I asked an experienced support worker, who had been at the centre for over 20 years, what was the common theme across the people he worked with. He didn't skip a beat and with a sense of inevitability he sighed 'childhood abuse'. I was taken aback by his certainty and the speed of his response.

The ACEs study pulls the anecdotal evidence together and puts it in a package that is hard to deny, that's the beauty of the ACEs study.

There are no voices of dissent and we can perhaps disagree on some aspects of the ACE phenomenon/movement but it's pretty hard to come away from it and think that this is not something that needs to be acted on. So, the next question is of course 'What can I do about ACEs?' and that is the big question that has rattled round my head since learning about ACEs. How do I take this very clear and simple message and use it to affect change?

One of the key rallying calls of the ACEs movement is that we are to support children to develop resilience. There are many definitions of resilience but in general they describe the ability to bounce back or continue to thrive following or during stress or adversity. I often hear people describe individuals as having a 'resilient personality' however The American psychological association (2017) counters that by explaining:

'Resilience is not a trait that people either have or do not have. It involves behaviours, thoughts and actions that can be learned and developed in anyone.' For children adversity can be compounded by the fact that their usual or anticipated supports, i.e. their parents, may be caught up in the same adversity and therefore unable to help them or worse the causes of that adversity.

The idea that resilience can be taught or modelled puts the focus on the adults around children who experience adversity to be available and to understand the implications of adversity on children.

Then to interact with children in a way that nurtures and promotes the development of children's resilience. There's been lots written on that and I'm not going to regurgitate it here but the foundation of that is positive relationships between children and adults. Kind, caring, listening, responsive, fun, responsible adults can be scarce on the ground for some children and we may be able to stand in that gap, even if it's for a few minutes or hours a day.

Thinking further about what we can do in relation to ACEs I've considered three areas; personal, professional and as a member of wider society

Personally

I have children and perhaps my circumstances are a little different to yours but as the adoptive father of six children, who the state decided could not and should not live with their biological parents, I see their ACEs very clearly. That may not be your story, but you may be a parent, grandparent, aunt, uncle, older sibling, or neighbour who comes in contact with children. In the first instance we need to speak to family and friends we need to share our knowledge and learning.

Adversity can be insidious and subtle we to need speak out when we see children in harm's way. That is a start, but we sometimes need to offer a helping hand. The possible circumstances are too many to list, but we can stand in the gap for children in our lives to be their voice and protect them. We can listen to children and be a safe haven for them and a smiling face.

The temptation is to speak in vague niceness's without specifics, but you know the children in your life, you know the nuances and subtleties of your family dynamics and relationships.

Professionally

We don't all work directly with children but for those that do we can consider the environment that we create around children and how we interact with children. Often when speaking with teachers we discuss the impact of trauma on behaviour. I describe to them, poor concentration, easily distracted, fidgeting, incessant talking, unresponsive or non-compliance as being frequent symptoms of traumatic experiences. We then reflect that the same list could be used when describing poor or challenging behaviour.

For those working with children the underlying issues are often hidden or masked by all manner of issues and it can take the wisdom of Solomon to decipher the truth. As professionals we should hold ACEs in mind as we work with children and consider it as a potential cause for some of the challenges that we may encounter. We can then consider our responses, can we offer a more compassionate and ACE informed environment for children, a safe and nurturing environment that facilitates growth and development or if necessary recovery and respite.

We don't all work directly with children in a learning environment, but we may come across children in our working day be that in healthcare, criminal justice, social care, retail, services etc. even if our contact with children is brief and intermittent we can demonstrate a safe and compassionate response to them and their needs. The child screaming in the checkout isle may have a lot more going on than we know or think.

Citizen of the wider society

Increasingly ACEs are being discussed in relation to public health policy and we may or may not be able to influence that directly through the work that we do. However, if you're over 18 you have a vote. If you believe the ACEs message you can in all fairness ask your elected politicians, be that councillors, MPs or Mayors, to consider how our budgets are spent, what the public health focus is and how we allocate our resources. We can raise the profile of the issues and force the debate.

Considering what we can and should do requires some thought and is influenced by our own experiences, circumstances and resources.

We all have limitations to what we can and can't do and some are able to directly influence children's circumstances.

Others aren't but can offer hope and kindness.

All views in this chapter are Al's own views and do not represent any business, charity or organisation that he is linked with.

8b. Judy James - What can YOU do about ACEs?

There is no 'one-size-fits-all' answer, but there are plenty of different options. A lived experience of toxic stress and an ACE score of 4 or more means that Yes, you were dealt a rough hand of cards in your early years, but that doesn't mean you have to keep the same hand for life; there are ways to change the face of the cards you hold so that you have a stronger more resilient hand to play going forward. Just like the grand masters of Poker, Bridge and similar card games, it may take the learning of new skills and repeated practice to gain mastery over the effects of your ACEs, but awareness, naming and taming emotion, as well as healing maladaptive responses, are all strategies that comprise a trump suit – a winning hand.

Trauma can be damaging and destructive, but it can also be the catalyst for transformation and change that results in positive outcomes. The brain shapes itself according to repeated experience, so therapeutic interventions that support the creation of new healthy and adaptive patterns can facilitate responsiveness in place of emotional reactivity.

Each individual is as unique as their lived experience, so there is no 'one-size-fits-all' therapy for treating the effects of ACEs.

It is known that relational and developmental trauma can have a negative lasting effect on physical health as well as mental health, so the psychological approach I adopt is integrative and uses interventions to work with the impact of complex trauma on the body as well as the mind and brain.

I believe it is essential to understand how the individual's body responds to trauma, to track how that impacts their executive functioning and action tendencies, and to support development of the body's capacity to calm and self-regulate.

Developmental trauma is an injury to the developing brain in childhood; it impairs social and emotional development, educational achievement and mental health. Therefore, I believe the psychological approach needs to be in line with the sequential process of child brain development, addressing the impact on different regions of the brain (the primitive, the limbic and the cortical regions) as well as how trauma impacts different types of memory – semantic, episodic, emotional and procedural.

There is a wide range of psychological approaches for the treatment of complex trauma, that is, chronic exposure to toxic stress that affects the physiology as well as psychological well-being. The range includes, but is not limited to: -

- Accelerated Experiential Dynamic Psychotherapy
- Attachment-Focused Therapy
- Body-Mind Psychotherapy
- Dialectical Behaviour Therapy
- Dyadic Developmental Psychotherapy
- Emotion-Focused Therapy (sometimes referred to as Process Experiential Therapy)
- Pesso Boyden System Psychomotor (PBSP)
- Somatic Experiencing
- Trauma Focused Cognitive Behavioural Therapy (TF-CBT)

Eye Movement Desensitisation Reprogramming (EMDR) can be effective for reprocessing memories of traumatic events: Episodic and more implicit emotional and somatic memories may also require a body-mind approach and potentially the integration of therapeutic life story work.

But what else can you do about ACEs?

Here are some of my thoughts: -

- Prevent them and prevent the inter-generational transmission of ACEs
- Take action now and intervene where you see occurrences of ACEs and Toxic Stress; there is a wealth of information now widely available about child development and how to support children and attend to their attachment needs by providing a safe haven and secure base.
- See behaviour as communication and recognise action tendencies as 'Stress behaviours', not mis-behaviour (stress behaviours being the result of distressing feelings that emanate from ACEs.)
- Participate in an ACEs forum or network - submit your ideas and be involved in collaboration to 'invent very wise actions' and build resilience.
- Be an 'Anybody' and do what anybody can do. I am referring to the anonymous rhyme about Everybody, Somebody, Anybody, Nobody: -

This is a little story about four people named Everybody, Somebody, Anybody, and Nobody.

There was an important job to be done and Everybody was sure that Somebody would do it.
Anybody could have done it, but Nobody did it.

Somebody got angry about that because it was Everybody's job.

Everybody thought that Anybody could do it, but Nobody realized that Everybody wouldn't do it.

It ended up that Everybody blamed Somebody when Nobody did what Anybody could have done.

Anybody can raise ACE awareness, intervene and help to invent wise actions. The prevention of ACEs and the need to address the long-term public health implications are important jobs to be done and they concern us all. Anybody and Everybody can be involved.

All views in this chapter are Judy's own views and do not represent any business, charity or organisation that she is linked with.

8c. Laura McConnell - What can you do about ACEs?

Creating a Culture of Kindness within our Schools
"If they don't experience it at home, the next place most children experience safety and kindness is school. Unless they don't." (Dr. Suzanne Zeedyck, Portobello Learning Festival, June 9th, 2018)

Most of us, if not all of us who work in education do it because we want to make a positive difference to the lives of the children and young people in our classes. We certainly did not get into teaching for the 'part-time hours' and never-ending holidays which many detractors of the profession often suggest; we are here because we care.

Stories of the good old days of education, halcyon days where children sat down nicely, listened well, got on with their work and never had mental health issues or neurological conditions such as Dyslexia, Autism or ADHD are often eulogised in staffrooms, on social media and in response to newspaper articles; glorious days when no one was in a rush to 'label' children with 'peculiar' conditions. Subsequently, the rise of video games, lack of outdoor play, social media intrusion, helicopter parenting, poor diet, decline of old-fashioned discipline and a lack of traditional parenting skills are often given as reasons for this crisis amongst our young people.

Whilst these factors may contribute, it is our increased understanding of Adverse Childhood Experiences (ACEs) and what it takes to foster resilience in children, combined with advances in our understanding of neurodevelopmental conditions that forms the real root of the increased diagnoses of these issues which are now being properly recognised.

Paradoxically, everyone also remembers the belt and Miss Trunchbull-type teachers who struck fear into our hearts for the most minor indiscretions, some of us remember being called stupid, weird or bad, and also feared the consequences at home if the teacher called; this was an everyday reality for many children in those classrooms of yore.

For many, the classroom of the past promoted a culture of fear which has, thankfully, dissipated as time has gone on, for most of our children. Rather than look through rose-tinted glasses at what we allegedly had, it would benefit everyone in education if teachers looked to the future and fostered a real compassion for children who may not be growing up in the idyll we pretend to remember.

Our society is such that ACEs are relatively common, but ACEs have always existed. In 'Resilience', directed by James Redford, a film that which is currently taking the world by storm, we learn that strong parental or adult buffering to ACEs is a key factor in building resilience amongst our young people, and I believe that building resilience is what we educators should look towards to improve lives of young people.

We should aim to be the 'Everyday Heroes' that Jaz Ampaw Farr talks about so powerfully in her Ted Talk of the same name. (Jaz Ampaw Farr, TEDxNorwichEd, 2017)

What can we do to improve the educational experience for all young people?

To fight a mental health crisis and to properly tackle ACEs comprehensively it will take a serious commitment from the government, the National Health Service, the Judicial System, the Police, Social Work and education; every single aspect of our society must work together. Inevitably, this will cost a lot of money which may or may not be available. Even if, or when, that money is made available, the radical social change required will take time if it is being directed by government, which is why I am so heartened by the grassroots ACEs' movement in Scotland, and that which is now emerging across England.

This grassroots movement is forging ahead of government and causing change by educating the masses who, in turn, are putting pressure on our politicians, and by reading this book you are part of that movement.

In the absence of a budget, can we really make a meaningful impact on children in schools? I would argue so and I would also argue that we can make that impact for free. In the same speech in which Dr. Suzanne Zeedyck made the comment I quoted at the opening of this chapter, she also talked about the pervading culture within many of our schools: whilst most children may appear, on the surface, to survive in an environment which is strict, controlling and populated with distant adults, the minority cannot survive or thrive in that environment at all and may stop attending school or become excluded. But, if you change the entire culture of the school to a "Culture of Kindness," then all of the children will be able to survive and thrive in a child-centred, caring and nurturing environment, with "no child left behind." Teachers may even enjoy working there too.

Kindness Costs Nothing

To improve the school environment for our young people, we do not need to spend a lot of money; in fact, we can make some very meaningful changes to the ethos of our schools for free. Where there is a budget, even more changes can be made that can positively affect the young people in our schools. However, let us assume there is no budget.

I recently heard Jim Roberson, Assistant Head of a large Secondary School on the South coast of England and author of 'The Discipline Coach', speak at a conference, and he said something which really resonated with me, "Show the young people that you want to be there." (Jim Roberson, Portobello Learning Festival, June 9th, 2018). If you come into school looking miserable and glum, looking like you would rather be at home in bed, then why would the young people want to get out of their beds and come to school? Why would they be happy there if they see miserable faces in the adults? Colleagues and I have often marvelled at how much children notice about us; if I wear eyeliner, change my nail polish or wear a dress they have never seen before the children comment on it.

Children notice the tiniest things about our appearance, the things that we have not paid much attention to ourselves, because they study us. They know if we want to be there or not.

It is because children study us that they know if we like them or not.

I once worked with a Depute Head who almost retreated every time she saw me approach in the corridor; she was hurried in her speech in order to demonstrate that she was very busy and never caught up with me when she promised she would, unless I insisted she did via email as it was essential for a child. There were other members of staff for whom she always had time, no matter how trivial the matter, and most importantly it was not just me who knew this; other staff members knew this too. It was humiliating, and I feared speaking to her in front of others.

People notice how you are treated by others and use that information to form judgements about you, particularly when it is someone in a leadership position, as a teacher is for young people. If we adults are aware when someone has no time for us and thinks of us as a nuisance, children must also know when we feel like that about them. More importantly, other children then use how we act to form judgements which affect their behaviour towards their peers If the teacher isolates a child with coldness then their peers are likely to as well. Children who grow up in an abusive environment, or those with neurodiverse conditions like ADHD which result in them being frequently chastised by adults, become hypervigilant about the adult behaviour around them.

They study your body language, facial expressions and your eyes, and while you might not be able to change your feelings about the child, please have an awareness of the way you act towards them because it is obvious to everyone.

If you do not like the children in your class, then they will not like you. You may view your role as one of raising attainment as opposed to being friends with the children and that is okay, but if that is your approach then remember the words of the late, great Rita Pierson who said, 'Kids don't learn from people they don't like.' (Rita Pierson, TED 2013).

In his book, 'When The Adults Change, Everything Changes' (a title which should be compulsory reading for all teachers), Paul Dix talks about a lot of simple cultural changes which can be made across a whole school which say "who we are" as a school. My favourite part of the book is when Paul Dix talks about replacing the thunderclouds and sunshine's, football pitches and red cards and those other visible behaviour systems with a recognition board. Growing up with ADHD, I could not help chatting in class, blurting out answers, fidgeting or being lost in my own thoughts, which in teacher speak is "not listening." Children who are living with trauma and do not know whether they will go home to sick parents, if there will be food to eat or do not know who will come into their bedroom that night find it really hard to concentrate in school.

They are on high alert and their emotions are not regulated; guess who finds their name on the thundercloud or the red card more than others? Get rid of the wall of shame and make it a wall of fame.

One of the most effective, free, ways of changing the culture of a school is pioneered by Head Teacher Jennifer Knussen and her team at a Primary School in Fife, Scotland. Their approach, which they call, "The Language of Connection," is beautifully effective in its simplicity. In that school, and in the others, who have heard them speak, they do not talk about 'challenging behaviour,' 'violent behaviour' or use words like 'naughty,' 'bad' or 'tricky'- they use the word 'distressed' instead. Changing that one simple word allows for a massive shift in our focus.

The children do not find their behaviour challenging or tricky; only the adults do. Yes, some distressed behaviour is challenging or even violent, but children are not an alien species sent to earth to make the lives of school staff difficult; they are little people, and no little person picks up a chair, turns over a table or screams and shouts and swears unless they are particularly distressed. Focus on the cause of that distress.

My favourite free approach to change the experience of children in school is to listen to them. I do not mean that we should just listen when something has happened.

I mean that we should be there to actively listen to children all the time. When children just have something to tell you about their lives, their weekends, when they have a question, check in with them every now and again and ask them what they have been doing recently.

By showing a genuine interest in their lives, remembering their dog's name or that they were excited to see their grandmother at the weekend, you demonstrate to the children that you see them and that you care about them. In turn, the children might actually ask you questions about your family, your hobbies or your pets (a favourite topic). For some children, that might be the only time someone has heard them that day or been interested in them as a person.

A colleague once told me that by telling the children my name, my age and stories about my life outside of school that I was 'overly familiar.' I remember screwing up my face and saying, "why can't we tell them our names? It's on our name badge dangling from our necks?" I still do not understand that attitude and nor do I want to; so, if faced with that kind of feedback from colleagues, then ask yourself if it is more important to build a respectful, trusting relationship with a child or to keep your name a secret for the sake of some strange familiarity code?

All of this is free to implement, it will not happen overnight but if you commit to changing your school into a culture of kindness then the children with ACEs who are suffering will benefit from it.

What not to do…

We teachers tend to operate at full throttle when we are given information about ways to help the children in our care, or when we find out about a new initiative that will make a difference.
However, after digesting information about ACEs and particularly after watching 'Resilience', I would urge a pause for reflection within the profession in the way that we might address the ACEs of the children in their care.

The obvious is probably not as obvious as you might think.

There is one particular strategy that I am asked about frequently, and one I am aware that some schools have forged ahead with: the practice of giving children 'ACE scores'. In my opinion, and I am not alone, this is a dangerously flawed practice for a variety of reasons, even if the intentions behind the practice are good.

As those of us who work in Rights Respecting Schools will know, Article 16 of the United Nations Convention on the Rights of the Child (UNCRC) states that children have 'the right to privacy'. I have seen many schools focus on children's diaries or social media when, in fact, it is about the child as a person and their right not to have everyone know about their lives. Key members of staff in each school benefit from knowing the details of a child's background, usually the Head Teacher or a Depute Head who is on a safeguarding list and the class teacher; however, only those who really need to know should be privy to a child's background information. Children deserve to live without judgement and backgrounds are not something that school staff are qualified to analyse or quantify. Even with the multi-agency 'Getting It Right For Every Child' (GIRFEC) approach which we have in Scotland, which involves children and their parents' in our Child Planning Process, we cannot possibly know enough about a child to confidently give them an ACE Score, and what would be the real purpose of education staff knowing children's ACE score anyway?

Let us not forget that ACE scores are an indicator for the potential health outcomes of those who suffered from trauma and the resulting long term toxic stress, they are not a list of criteria by which we can judge children's social or educational outcomes or where resources should be directed.

Children with four identified ACEs may have additional health risk indicators but do not necessarily need to be 'flagged up' for additional input in comparison to children with three identified ACEs; what about the children with no identified ACEs? The word identified is key there. Presented with what we now know, and with an awareness of how prevalent ACEs are and the way they can touch every one of us, the best approach we can adopt in education is to change our ethos and approach to all children. Let us adopt that culture of kindness which allows our children to feel safe, happy and nurtured in school. It will not just do wonders for their mental health but also their attainment.

All views in this chapter are Laura's own views and do not represent any business, charity or organisation that she is linked with.

References

Ampaw Farr, J (2017) The Power of Everyday Heroes [Video File]. Available at. https://www.youtube.com/watch?v=q3xoZXSW5yc

Dix, P (2017) When The Adults Change, Everything Changes, Independent Thinking Press

Pierson, R (2013) Every Kid Needs a Champion [Video File]. Available at. https://www.youtube.com/watch?v=SFnMTHhKdkw

Resilience: The Biology of Stress and the Science of Hope, (2016) [film], Directed by James REDFORD. USA. KPJR Films

Roberson, J (2012) The Discipline Coach, Independent Thinking Press

Roberson, J (2018) 'Discipline is Not What You Do to Yourself, But For Yourself- a guide to relationship building.' presented at the Portobello Learning Festival Conference 9th June, Edinburgh

Zeedyck, S (2018) 'Setting the Challenge: the science and reality of adverse childhood experiences' presented at the Portobello Learning Festival Conference 9th June, Edinburgh

8d. A Survivor – What can YOU do about ACEs?

ACEs prevention and reduction.

Adverse childhood experiences (ACEs) can often create dangerous levels of stress in children and can negatively affect healthy brain development, which can then cause bad long-term effects on a young person's learning ability, behaviour and health.

Neurobiological research indicates that 'toxic stress', the bad version of stress, which is defined as the 'prolonged activation of stress response systems in the absence of protective relationships', is associated with ACEs and can lead to physical changes in the way the child's brain develops. Bad stuff can literally change brain development, altering how it works and responds to the World around it.

Fortunately, the brain is 'plastic', not literally, but just like plastic it can be reshaped.

Despite any level of ACEs that are endured in childhood, the brain is not fixed in a negative state and lost forever; there is a lot that can be done to respond in a psychologically informed way. The role of adults, including parents, teachers and all care sector and support staff across society is therefore crucial in the prevention and reduction of ACEs.

Many Children with a high ACEs score do go on to do well despite their childhood adversity. They are the children who have usually had at least one stable, caring, loving, committed relationship with a supportive parent, or caregiver. This may have been a family member, a neighbour, even a football coach (of the non-predatory variety).

Having this type of person in a young life can rebalance the fulcrum and help build skills such as the ability to plan, monitor and regulate behaviour and adapt to the changing circumstances in their lives. It's called resilience, learning to bounce back. The capacity to recover quickly from difficulties caused by adverse childhood experiences.

Toxic stress caused by adverse childhood experiences literally affects our physiology, the functions and activities of our human life and living matter such as our bodies organs, tissues, and cells. Toxic stress can undermine the ability to form meaningful relationships, regulate our emotions, and can seriously impair our cognitive functions.

So, in plain language, how can we prevent and reduce ACEs?

I guess preventing them is impossible. We live in a world that is creating adversity at so many levels it would be naïve to think we can eradicate them all.

In my view, and after reading many articles about what can be done, it boils down to relatively uncomplicated actions. An immediate change in mind-set and approach will go a long way to combating ACEs.

If we know about ACEs and we accept the science, then we know that doing something is better than doing nothing. Whatever the something is, it will have the power to reduce the ACEs and the effect on young lives.

If we asked a GP to write a wonderful life changing prescription that would reduce ACEs, it may read something like this;

'Take a global look at the child's life, every part of it. Recognise the parts that are causing the ACEs symptoms. Recognise signs of physical or emotional neglect. This may include bad diet, poor living conditions, and levels of poverty.

Take a look at the adults in the child's life. They may be caring loving parents who are suffering from mental ill health, illicit substance abuse, or simply struggling to find work and pay their bills. They may have ACEs themselves. The child may live in a relatively well equipped clean home, but they may also be getting bullied at school or by siblings or they may be physically, sexually, or emotionally abused by others in the household, the local neighbourhood, or even at school or church.

Take a close look at the family and the environment around the child and look for signs of household dysfunction.

After assessing the child's global circumstances, take several doses of love and concern, add this to as many practical acts of support you can muster and repeat on a daily basis. Help build resilience at every opportunity. Change the conversation with everyone from 'what's wrong with you? to 'what happened to you?'

I know this sounds simplistic, it is just my view. I am sure you will gain invaluable insight from other sources, including Al Coates, Judy James and Laura McConnell.

If you have not done so already, please listen very carefully to Dr Nadine Burke Harris's TEDMED Talk.

Better still, go and buy her book; The Deepest Well. I recommend this book to everyone. In, The Deepest Well, Dr Burke Harris reveals the science behind childhood adversity and offers a new way of understanding the adverse events that affect us throughout our lifetime.

Based on her own ground-breaking clinical work and public leadership, Dr Burke Harris shows us how we can disrupt this cycle through interventions that help retrain the brain and body, foster resilience, and help children, families, and adults live healthier, happier lives.

The good news is, the earlier you can identify that a child is experiencing ACEs and toxic stress, the sooner children and families can be connected to the services they need to prevent or heal the effects.

http://www.adversechildhoodexperiences.co.uk/dr-nadine-burke-harris

I have nothing to gain by recommending Dr Nadine Burke Harris's book - apart from the good feeling that I have done something worthwhile.

ACEs sustainable recovery.

The first time I heard the phrase 'sustainable recovery' was when I first had peer support from Graham Wilmer MBE.

Having recognised that there is an identifiable, comorbid psychological disorder that develops in survivors of sexual abuse, Graham and his colleagues set about developing a holistic recovery framework that could be offered to survivors of all ages, which would help them reach a point that they call a sustainable recovery; a point from which they would not regress.

The recovery model he developed is in line with the criteria set down by the government for ISVAs (Independent Sexual Violence Advisors), which meets the requirements of Best Evidence Practice, and enables the victims to withstand the rigours of being a prosecution witness.

Some may argue against this model of sustainable recovery, but I don't really care for their argument. I know it works.

For me, the journey of sustainable recovery started with Graham Wilmer's peer support and continued with the range of therapies and self-education I have previously outlined. It has been and remains a truly holistic experience for me.

Sustainable recovery from ACEs is a no-brainer (pardon the pun).

I do still have moments when something triggers my low mood. Sometimes I get caught up in my own negative ruminations, and they affect my productivity. Sometimes I misread signals from other people, and sometimes I need a glass of wine (or 3) to help me relax.

Most of the time however, now I have had the therapy, peer support, self-education, medication, and love from my family, I usually recover very quickly.

I am human, and I feel pain, my own and others. If I cry, then I cry, who cares? It's human to cry. I am normal if pain and suffering, my own or others, ignites empathetic responses.

I am not a china doll that needs wrapping in foam to avoid breakages. People who have endured ACEs are probably emotionally tougher and more resilient than those few in society without ACEs.

You do not have to dance around the conversation about sexual abuse or any other ACE. It's a sad fact of life that needs exposure. I find most people stumble with the words and they are themselves embarrassed and too frightened to talk about ACEs.

Don't get me wrong, I am sensitive to other people's feelings and views, as we all should be, but at the same time I think being sensitive and gentle and politically correct is often a waste of time. Get to the f**king point and deal with it.

The term 'ACEs' is a convenient and very palatable expression we can all use in good company, but let's not forget that behind this polite little acronym are the real lives of children and adults blighted by insult, humiliation, fear, physical injury, threat, child sexual abuse and exploitation, rejection, poverty, alcoholism, divorce, abandonment, drug abuse, mental health issues, suicide, and imprisonment; to name just a few shades of ACEs.

We need to deal with this human crisis that lies at the foot of so much suffering.

My own ACEs sustained recovery is evidenced by the increasing gaps between annual meltdowns, habitual negative rumination, inappropriate repeated fight, flight and freeze responses, and the ability to love and trust others. (Most of the time).

I have had to face my ACEs looking them looking square in the eye. No amount of dancing or pussyfooting around them was going to cut the mustard.

It was Graham Wilmer who first shocked me into dealing with the harsh reality when he said to me, during a peer support session 'so, what you are saying is; one bastard raped you repeatedly when you were a child, another one beat the shit out of you, and your mother just abandoned you'.

From that day I have stopped pulling punches and dressing my ACEs up, so they are more palatable for everyone else, I now describe them as they were in my reality; when I am in adult company that is and it's appropriate to do so.

My body has a full set of ACEs induced symptoms. A life blighted by ACEs has caused changes in function and effectiveness of my brain and in my body's neurology.

The result? A range of specific, identifiable illnesses and conditions such as pain, anguish, and trauma. These things have been making me sick for a long time.

My medical records report a wide array of symptoms and health outcomes, some through mental health analysis, and others through physical examination and tests.

I have mild IBS, duodenal and gastric ulcers, constant headaches and tinnitus. I also have Wolf-Parkinson-White (WPW) syndrome. I also suffer from bouts of debilitating fatigue. None of these conditions are directly caused by ACEs (as far as I know) but the ACEs science shows significant evidence that ACEs can considerably hinder or exacerbate these conditions.

Around the age of 9 I was diagnosed with Erythema Nodosum and Thrombophlebitis (blood clotting) which appears to have been a psychosomatic physical condition and CPTSD symptom caused by Adverse Childhood Experiences (ACEs).

At the height of the physical abuse I was enduring when aged 10, a doctor recorded that despite observation and exhaustive investigation he was unable able to call my condition anything other than 'idiopathic' (spontaneous and the cause unknown), another doctor recorded in his notes that it was probably caused by trauma.

It's important to understand that ACEs are a powerful determinant of who we become as adults – in behaviour and in health. The more ACEs we experience the greater potential of the impact on our health later in life.

This is because the cumulative impact of trauma builds up, so the higher the ACEs score we have, the greater the risk of us developing more and more serious, health conditions later in life.

So, many chronic diseases we have as adults have their origins in our adverse childhood experiences. Autoimmune diseases, cancer, heart disease, stroke – as well as mental health conditions and risky behaviour can all be traced back to ACEs for many people.

I have a body that delivers pain in most of my joints daily and often I have debilitating back pain that regularly takes me to my knees in tears and expletives. I struggle with my weight and my mental health has always been edging on the side of fragile, even though I am considered as high-functioning and creative.

My depressive bouts are commonly referred to as dysthymia, or Persistent Depressive Disorder (PDD). It carries all the same symptoms of major depression but it's a lot harder to spot and I have suffered it most of my life, and mostly in silence.

As my eminent Professor has recently confirmed, I have a 'complex Post-Traumatic Stress Disorder of a relatively severe and very chronic nature with a recurrent depressive disorder which is longstanding and has been severe'.

As a child I failed to engage with the other boys in school, or the teachers, often spending hours staring in silence out of the window and unable to participate in school activities and lessons.

At an even younger age the abuse included levels of threat and violence from an alcoholic step-parent; causing mental health and behaviour issues and somatic symptoms such as loss of speech and visual disturbances. I can't be sure if my loss of speech was a deliberate act or a trauma response.

Unusual either way.

What did the idiots in charge of my childhood do about these health issues?

Very little.

I had a high ACEs score of around 7 that was obvious when I was aged 5, and no one noticed or even cared. The final count up to 10 ACEs was scored just after I was raped and sexually assaulted by the people charged by social services with my rehabilitation and care.

Ironic I know.

The child may not remember but the body does.

I remember most of my ACEs from age 5 onwards.
My DNA remembers everything.

So, that is what my 'sustainable recovery' is recovering from.

A shed-load of full-on shit that missed a variety of fans during my first 15 years of childhood hitting me square in the face and leaving an indelible mark in the shadows of my life.

Full-on shit (technical term for ACEs) which my eminent Professor says I am: 'Unlikely to ever make a complete recovery from'.

It's my sustainable recovery, and I am happy to hold on to it.

Thank you, Graham Wilmer MBE.

I hope this little book has provided a helpful insight into the little acronym known as ACEs.

I also hope you now see the importance for everyone in our society to understand adverse childhood experiences, the biology of stress and the science of hope.

Whatever you do about ACEs, do it with love.

Love conquers all.

Final words.

I will leave you with more wise words that are not mine. The following is an excerpt from a blog entitled: 8 ways people recover from post childhood adversity syndrome. by Donna Jackson Nakazawa, published on the https://acestoohigh.com website - which has an abundance of ACEs related information for your further research.

The very first book I read, that started to make sense of my own ACEs journey was Childhood Disrupted, How Your Biography Becomes Your Biology And How You Can Heal, written by Donna Jackson Nakazawa. That book sown seeds of understanding in my mind that Dr Nadine Burke-Harris later watered for me.

After reading Donna's book twice over I gave it to one of my sisters in the hope that this new-found wisdom would help her like it had started to help me.

I chose this particular blog from the thousands of articles and blogs available on the internet because I found it to be concise, and straightforward.

It was published in September 2016, when most of us in the UK had never heard of ACEs, and it demonstrates that we have some catching up to do here in the UK. The blog, like her book, brings invaluable knowledge and guidance from our colleagues in the USA who we can thank for the original ACEs research and the subsequent world-wide ACEs awareness movement that has no doubt shaken things up and brought understanding and hope to thousands of people who may never have made the connection between their own adverse childhood experiences and the negative mental and physical health outcomes they have been enduring for too long.

There is truth to the old saying that knowledge is power. Once you understand that your body and brain have been harmed by the biological impact of early emotional trauma, you can at last take the necessary, science-based steps to remove the fingerprints that early adversity left on your neurobiology. You can begin a journey to healing, to reduce your proclivity to inflammation, depression, addiction, physical pain, and disease.

Science tells us that biology does not have to be destiny. ACEs can last a lifetime, but they don't have to.

We can reboot our brains. Even if we have been set on high reactive mode for decades or a lifetime, we can still dial it down. We can respond to life's inevitable stressors more appropriately and shift away from an overactive inflammatory response. We can become neurobiologically resilient. We can turn bad epigenetics into good epigenetics and rescue ourselves.

Today, researchers recognise a range of promising approaches to help create new neurons (known as neurogenesis), make new synaptic connections between those neurons (known as synaptogenesis), promote new patterns of thoughts and reactions, bring under-connected areas of the brain back online—and reset our stress response so that we decrease the inflammation that makes us ill.

We have the capacity, within ourselves, to create better health. We might call this brave undertaking "the neurobiology of awakening."

There can be no better time than now to begin your own awakening, to proactively help yourself and those you love, embrace resilience, and move forward toward growth, even transformation.

Here are some steps to try:

Take the ACE questionnaire.

The single most important step you can take toward healing and transformation is to fill out the ACE questionnaire for yourself and share your results with your health-care practitioner.

For many people, taking the 10-question survey "helps to normalize the conversation about adverse childhood experiences and their impact on our lives," says Vincent Felitti, co-founder of the CDC-Kaiser Permanente ACE Study. "When we make it okay to talk about what happened, it removes the power that secrecy so often has."

You're not asking your healthcare practitioner to act as your therapist, or to change your prescriptions; you're simply acknowledging that there might be a link between your past and your present. Ideally, given the recent discoveries in the field of ACEs research, your doctor should acknowledge that this link is plausible, and add some of the following modalities to your healing protocol.

Begin writing to heal.

Think about writing down your story of childhood adversity, using a technique psychologists call "writing to heal." James Pennebaker, professor of psychology at the University of Texas, Austin, developed this assignment, which demonstrates the effects of writing as a healing modality. He suggests: "Over the next four days, write down your deepest emotions and thoughts about the emotional upheaval that has been influencing your life the most. In your writing, really let go and explore the event and how it has affected you.

You might tie this experience to your childhood, your relationship with your parents, people you have loved or love now...Write continuously for twenty minutes a day."

When Pennebaker had students complete this assignment, their grades went up. When adults wrote to heal, they made fewer doctors' visits and demonstrated changes in their immune function.

The exercise of writing about your secrets, even if you destroy what you've written afterward, has been shown to have positive health effects.

Practice mindfulness meditation.

A growing body of research indicates that individuals who've practiced mindfulness meditation and mindfulness-based stress reduction (MBSR) show an increase in grey matter in the same parts of the brain that are damaged by adverse childhood experiences and shifts in genes that regulate their physiological stress response.

According to Trish Magyari, LCPC, a mindfulness-based psychotherapist and researcher who specializes in trauma and illness, adults suffering from PTSD due to childhood sexual abuse who took part in a "trauma-sensitive" MBSR program, had less anxiety and depression, and demonstrated fewer PTSD symptoms, even two years after taking the course.

Many meditation centres offer MBSR classes and retreats, but you can practice anytime in your own home. Choose a time and place to focus on your breath as it enters and leaves your nostrils; the rise and fall of your chest; the sensations in your hands or through the whole body; or sounds within or around you. If you get distracted, just come back to your anchor. Here are some tips from Tara Brach, psychologist and meditation teacher, to get you started on your mindfulness journey.

There are many medications you can take that dampen the sympathetic nervous system (which ramps up your stress response when you come into contact with a stressor), but there aren't any medications that boost the parasympathetic nervous system (which helps to calm your body down after the stressor has passed). Your breath is the best natural calming treatment—and it has no side effects.

Yoga

When children face ACEs, they often store decades of physical tension from a fight, flight, or freeze state of mind in their bodies. PET scans show that yoga decreases blood flow to the amygdala, the brain's alarm centre, and increases blood flow to the frontal lobe and prefrontal cortex, which help us to react to stressors with a greater sense of equanimity. Yoga has also been found to increase levels of GABA—or gamma-aminobutyric acid—a chemical that improves brain function, promotes calm, and helps to protect us against depression and anxiety.

Therapy

Sometimes, the long-lasting effects of childhood trauma are just too great to tackle on our own. In these cases, says Jack Kornfield, psychologist and meditation teacher, "meditation is not always enough." We need to bring unresolved issues into a therapeutic relationship and get back-up in unpacking the past. When we partner with a skilled therapist to address the adversity we may have faced decades ago, those negative memories become paired with the positive experience of being seen by someone who accepts us as we are— and a new window to healing opens.

Part of the power of therapy lies in allowing ourselves, finally, to form an attachment to a safe person. A therapist's unconditional acceptance helps us to modify the circuits in our brain that tell us that we can't trust anyone, and grow new, healthier neural connections. It can also help us to heal the underlying, cellular damage of traumatic stress, down to our DNA. In one study, patients who underwent therapy showed changes in the integrity of their genome—even a year after their regular sessions ended.

EEG neurofeedback

Electroencephalographic (EEG) neurofeedback is a clinical approach to healing childhood trauma in which patients learn to influence their thoughts and feelings by watching their brain's electrical activity in real-time, on a laptop screen. Someone hooked up to the computer via electrodes on his scalp might see an image of a field; when his brain is under-activated in a key area, the field, which changes in response to neural activity, may appear to be muddy and grey, the flowers wilted; but when that area of the brain reactivates, it triggers the flowers to burst into colour and birds to sing. With practice, the patient learns to initiate certain thought patterns that lead to neural activity associated with pleasant images and sounds.

You might think of a licensed EEG neurofeedback therapist as a musical conductor, who's trying to get different parts of the orchestra to play a little more softly in some cases, and a little louder in others, in order to achieve harmony.

After just one EEG neurofeedback session, patients showed greater neural connectivity and improved emotional resilience, making it a compelling option for those who've suffered the long-lasting effects of chronic, unpredictable stress in childhood.

EMDR therapy

Eye movement desensitization and reprocessing (EMDR) is a potent form of psychotherapy that helps individuals to remember difficult experiences safely and relate those memories in ways that no longer cause pain in the present. Here's how it works: EMDR-certified therapists help patients to trigger painful emotions. As these emotions lead the patients to recall specific difficult experiences, they are asked to shift their gaze back and forth rapidly, often by following a pattern of lights or a wand that moves from right to left, right to left, in a movement that simulates the healing action of REM sleep.

The repetitive directing of attention in EMDR induces a neurobiological state that helps the brain to re-integrate neural connections that have been dysregulated by chronic, unpredictable stress and past experiences. This re-integration can, in turn, lead to a reduction in the episodic, traumatic memories we store in the hippocampus, and downshift the amygdala's activity. Other studies have shown that EMDR increases the volume of the hippocampus.

EMDR therapy has been endorsed by the World Health Organization as one of only two forms of psychotherapy for children and adults in natural disasters and war settings

Rally community healing

Often, ACEs stem from bad relationships—neglectful relatives, schoolyard bullies, abusive partners—but the right kinds of relationships can help to make us whole again. When we find people who support us, when we feel "tended and befriended," our bodies and brains have a better shot at healing. Research has found that having strong social ties improves outcomes for women with breast cancer, multiple sclerosis, and other diseases. In part, that's because positive interactions with others boost our production of oxytocin, a "feel-good" hormone that dials down the inflammatory stress response. If you're at a loss for ways to connect, try a mindfulness meditation community or an MBSR class, or pass along the ACE questionnaire or even my newest book, Childhood Disrupted: How Your Biography Becomes Your Biology, and How You Can Heal, to family and friends to spark important, meaningful conversations.

You're not alone

Whichever modalities you and your physician choose to implement, it's important to keep in mind that you're not alone. When you begin to understand that your feelings of loss, shame, guilt, anxiety, or grief are shared by so many others, you can lend support and swap ideas for healing.

When you embrace the process of healing despite your adverse childhood experiences, you don't just become who you might have been if you hadn't encountered childhood suffering in the first place. You gain something better—the hard-earned gift of life wisdom, which you bring forward into every arena of your life.

The recognition that you have lived through hard times drives you to develop deeper empathy, seek more intimacy, value life's sweeter moments, and treasure your connectedness to others and to the world at large. This is the hard-won benefit of having known suffering. Best of all, you can find ways to start right where you are, no matter where you find yourself.

Donna Jackson Nakazawa is an award-winning science journalist interested in exploring the intersection between neuroscience, immunology, and the deepest inner workings of the human heart. She studied English and Public Policy at Duke University and is a graduate of Harvard's Radcliffe program in publishing.□

Links for further research and information.

Search 'ACEs' or 'Adverse Childhood Experiences' in any search engine and you will find information from around the world.
Here is a random selection;

http://www.adversechildhoodexperiences.co.uk/

https://www.cdc.gov/violenceprevention/acestudy/index

https://www.blackburn.gov.uk/Pages/aces.aspx

http://www.healthscotland.scot/population-groups/children/adverse-childhood-experiences

https://beta.gov.scot/publications/adverse-childhood-experiences/

http://www.wales.nhs.uk/sitesplus/888/page/88524

https://www.scottishrecovery.net/addressing-adverse-childhood-experiences-in-scotland/

http://www.aces.me.uk/in-wales/

http://www.cph.org.uk/case-study/adverse-childhood-experiences-aces/

http://www.70-30.org.uk/18737-2/

https://acestoohigh.com/got-your-ace-score/

https://www.ncjfcj.org/sites/default/files/Finding%20Your%20ACE%20Score.pdf

http://buncombeaces.org/your-ace-score/

https://www.gla.ac.uk/researchinstitutes/healthwellbeing/research/mentalhealth/research/projects/acecentre/

http://www.aceresponse.org/

ACEs Training (UK)

When I first discovered the science of Adverse Childhood Experiences I immediately started looking for ACEs awareness training that I could affordably access here in the UK.

I was hungry for knowledge.

After a few days of frustrating internet searching, back at the beginning of the year, I was disappointed with the results.

I did find some ACEs training, but not much, and most priced beyond my reach, one wanting £500 for a 2-day course.

I did an online course based in the USA that cost around $40 but it was very basic.

More recently I have noticed that ACEs related training and ACEs related awareness conferences have started to emerge from a wide variety of services across the UK.

I have recently attended a few of these ACEs related training/conferences.

Following on from my original search frustrations, I decided to approach my friend Joanne Caffrey from www.totaltrain.co.uk and I asked if she would help me devise ACEs training that could be accredited and accessible without huge cost implications for those attending.

Joanne was a Police Officer for 24 years, during which time she spent 17 years as a sergeant and held a variety of roles including: Sex offences investigator, Custody sergeant., Patrol sergeant., Tactical support group sergeant (i.e. riot & public disorder), Training department sergeant, head of specialist police training, Civil contingencies / emergency planning sergeant (including counter terrorism security advice, event planning and VIP visits). She is also an NSPCC trained trainer and NFPS licensed centre for child protection & safeguarding.

Together we have now created CPD (Continued Professional Development) accredited ACEs training that will be available by September 2018.

The 1-day course will be designed for delegates who are working with children, young people, or adults in education, care, or custody settings, as well as parents, survivors, and practitioners with an interest in adverse childhood experiences.

The training will enable you to:

Identify the ACEs (Adverse Childhood Experiences) used in the CDC-Kaiser ACEs Study
Identify how ACEs affect long-term health
Identify what can be done to prevent ACEs
Identify how to screen for ACEs and support recovery from ACEs, and how to build resilience
Identify the basics of Neuroplasticity

If you would like to know more about this training, please visit:

http://www.adversechildhoodexperiences.co.uk/aces-training

Adverse Childhood Experience (ACE) Questionnaire

While you were growing up, during your first 18 years of life:

1. Did a parent or other adult in the household OFTEN:
- swear at you, insult you, put you down, or humiliate you?
- Or act in a way that made you afraid that you might be physically hurt?
- Or did other children, including brothers and sisters, OFTEN hit you, threaten you, pick on you or insult you?

Yes   or   No   If yes enter 1 [ ]

----

2. Did a parent or other adult in the household OFTEN:
- push, grab, slap, or throw something at you (other than spanking)?
- Or ever hit you so hard that you had marks or were injured?

Yes   or   No   If yes enter 1 [ ]

----

3. Did an adult or person at least 5 years older than you EVER:
- touch or fondle you or have you touch their body in a sexual way?
- Or try to or actually have oral, anal, or vaginal sex with you?

Yes   or   No   If yes enter 1 [ ]

----

4. Did you OFTEN feel:
- that no one in your family loved you or thought you were important or special?
- Or that your family didn't look out for each other, feel close to each other, or support each other?

- Or lonely, rejected or that nobody liked you?

Yes   or   No   If yes enter 1 [ ]

---

5.   Did you OFTEN feel that:
- you didn't have enough to eat, had to wear dirty clothes, and had no one to protect you?
- Or that your parents were too drunk or high to take care of you or take you to the doctor if you needed it?
- Or was there a period of 2 years or more where your family was very poor or unable to afford necessities like food and clothes?

Yes   or   No   If yes enter 1 [ ]

---

6.   Was a biological parent EVER lost to you through divorce, abandonment or any other reason?

Yes   or   No   If yes enter 1 [ ]

---

7.   Was your parent or carer OFTEN:
- pushed, grabbed, slapped, or had something thrown at him/her?
- Or SOMETIMES or OFTEN kicked, bitten, hit with a fist, or hit with something hard?
- Or EVER repeatedly hit over at least a few minutes or threatened with a gun or knife?
- Or did you live for 2 years or more in a neighbourhood that was dangerous or where you saw people being assaulted?

Yes   or   No   If yes enter 1 [ ]

---

8.   Did you live with anyone who was a problem drinker or alcoholic or who used street drugs?

Yes   or   No   If yes enter 1 [ ]

---

9. Was a household member depressed or mentally ill or did a household member attempt suicide?
Yes   or   No   If yes enter 1 [ ]

---

10. Did a household member go to prison?
Yes   or   No   If yes enter 1 [ ]

Now add up your "Yes" answers. This is your ACE Score [ ]

The most important thing to remember is that the ACE score is meant as a guideline:

If you experienced other types of toxic stress over months or years, then those would likely increase your risk of health consequences.

Visit: https://acestoohigh.com/got-your-ace-score/   to find out more about ACEs scoring and check out your Resilience Score.

I believe the most important thing you can do is to reframe how you see, understand, and respond to physical and mental illness and behaviours, both with yourself, your family, your colleagues, and the children or adults you support.

Many will have mental and physical health outcomes that are directly related to ACEs.

Like it says in the RESILIENCE film:

We need to change the conversation from
'What's wrong with you?' to 'What happened to you'.
www.adversechildhoodexperiences.co.uk

Made in the USA
Lexington, KY
23 August 2018